THE Athenian Agora
Site Guide

THE Athenian Agora Site Guide

FIFTH EDITION

John McK. Camp II

with photographs by
Craig A. Mauzy

THE AMERICAN SCHOOL OF CLASSICAL STUDIES AT ATHENS
PRINCETON, NEW JERSEY

Copyright 2010. The American School of Classical Studies at Athens.
All rights reserved.

Book design and layout: Mary Jane Gavenda

Library of Congress Cataloging-in-Publication Data
Camp, John McK.
    The Athenian Agora : site guide / by John McK. Camp II ; with photographs by Craig A. Mauzy.
—5th ed.
        p.   cm.
    Previous ed. cataloged under title: Athenian Agora : a guide to the excavation and museum.
    Includes index.
    ISBN 978-0-87661-657-4 (alk. paper)
    1. Agora (Athens, Greece) 2. Athens (Greece)—Antiquities. 3. Greece—Antiquities. I. Camp,
John McK. II. Mauzy, Craig A. III. Title.
NA283.A27A43 2010
914.95′12—dc22   2009044168

Printed in Italy

Table of Contents

FOREWORD

THIS IS THE FIFTH EDITION OF THE AGORA GUIDE. Many parts have been retained from the earlier editions by M. L. Lang and C. W. J. Eliot (1954), H. A. Thompson (1962, 1976), and J. McK. Camp II (1990). The present guide takes account of new discoveries and recent scholarship. It is intended for visitors actually touring the site and is arranged topographically, monument by monument. A general plan, with the individual buildings numbered, is in a pocket at the back of the book and cross-referenced in the text as ⓪. For a thematic account of the site, see H. A. Thompson and R. E. Wycherley, *The Agora of Athens* (*Agora* XIV, 1972), and for a historical approach, see J. McK. Camp II, *The Athenian Agora* (London, 1986). This guide concerns the antiquities and monuments on the site; in order to keep the size and weight appropriate for the visitor, a separate guide will be produced for the Agora Museum, housed in the Stoa of Attalos. (The icon Ⓜ in this guide highlights artifacts usually on display.)

Short bibliographic notes 🔖 are provided at the end of many entries for the visitor who may wish to know more about an individual monument.

At the end of the book, the reader will find a list of the publications of the American School of Classical Studies at Athens that specifically concern material recovered from the Agora. Digital versions of a number of publications, and many other resources, are available through the Web site of the Agora excavations, http://www.ascsa.edu.gr/agora.

This edition is the first to make use of color images, taken by Craig A. Mauzy. Archival images were taken by a succession of Agora photographers: Alison Frantz, James Heyle, Eugene Vanderpool Jr., Robert K. Vincent, and Craig A. Mauzy. Most of the drawings are the work of successive staff architects: John Travlos, William B. Dinsmoor Jr., and Richard Anderson.

Work in the Athenian Agora is sponsored by the American School of Classical Studies at Athens and the Packard Humanities Institute, with support from Randolph-Macon College, the Samuel H. Kress Foundation, and individual donors. The results described here were accomplished by hundreds of individuals. The views expressed are based on the combined thinking of the many scholars who have worked at the Agora excavations for almost 80 years.

John McK. Camp II, Director, Agora Excavations

HISTORY AND TIMELINE

PREHISTORY AND PROTOHISTORY (3000–700 B.C.)	ARCHAIC PERIOD (700–480 B.C.)	CLASSICAL PERIOD (480–323 B.C.)

ca. 3000 B.C.
Late Neolithic period.
Earliest recorded habitation in Athens on the Acropolis slopes.

3000–1550 B.C.
Early and Middle Helladic periods.

1550–1100 B.C.
Mycenaean period (Late Helladic or Late Bronze Age).
Period of Greek mythology: fall of Troy; *Odyssey*; Jason and the Argonauts; Theseus and the Minotaur.

1100–700 B.C.
Protogeometric and Geometric periods (Iron Age).
Period of Greek colonization/migration; Olympic games start, 776 B.C.; introduction of the alphabet.

ca. 600 B.C.
Lawgiver Solon (594 B.C.), beginnings of Athenian democracy.

560–510 B.C.
Rule of the tyrant Peisistratos and his sons Hippias and Hipparchos. Assassination of Hipparchos, 514 B.C.

508/7 B.C.
Creation of Athenian democracy under Kleisthenes.

490–479 B.C.
Persian Wars: Battles of Marathon (490 B.C.), Thermopylai (480 B.C.), Salamis (480 B.C.), and Plataia (479 B.C.). Athens destroyed by Persians, 480 B.C.

460–429 B.C.
Age of Perikles, rise of Athens.

431–404 B.C.
Peloponnesian War, Athens versus Sparta (Peace of Nikias, 421–415 B.C.)

399 B.C.
Death of Sokrates.

338 B.C.
Rise of Macedon under Philip II and Alexander; Battle of Chaironeia (338 B.C.); Lykourgos in charge of Athenian finances, 338–326 B.C.

323 B.C.
Death of Alexander the Great.

| HELLENISTIC PERIOD (323–86 B.C.) | ROMAN PERIOD (86 B.C.–A.D. 529) | BYZANTINE AND LATER (A.D. 530 +) |

3rd century B.C.
Macedonian occupation of Athens.

159–138 B.C.
Building of the Stoa of Attalos, funded by Attalos II, king of Pergamon.

146 B.C.
Ascendancy of Rome in Greece. Sack of Corinth by Mummius.

86 B.C.
Siege and capture of Athens by the Roman general Sulla.

27 B.C.–A.D. 14
Reign of Augustus.

A.D. 117–138
Reign of Hadrian.

A.D. 138–161
Reign of Antoninus Pius.

ca. A.D. 150
Visit of Pausanias to Athens.

A.D. 267
Athens and the Agora burned by the Herulians.

A.D. 330
Founding of Constantinople.

A.D. 396
Invasion of Athens by Visigoths under Alaric; some damage to the Agora.

A.D. 529
Schools of Athens closed by the emperor Justinian.

A.D. 582/3
Devastation probably caused by Slavs; abandonment of the Agora.

10th/11th century A.D.
Reoccupation of Agora area; Church of the Holy Apostles built.

A.D. 1204
Lower city of Athens devastated by Leon Sgouros from Nauplia.

A.D. 1456–1458
Capture of Athens by the Ottomans (lower city, A.D. 1456; Acropolis, A.D. 1458).

A.D. 1687
Venetian siege and bombardment of the Acropolis.

A.D. 1821–1828
Greek War of Independence. Two sieges of the Acropolis.

A.D. 1834
Athens becomes the capital of modern Greece.

INTRODUCTION

CLASSICAL ATHENS SAW THE RISE of an achievement unparalleled in history. Perikles, Aeschylus, Sophocles, Plato, Demosthenes, Thucydides, and Praxiteles are just a few of the statesmen and playwrights, historians and artists, philosophers and orators who flourished here during the 4th and 5th centuries B.C., when Athens was the most powerful city-state in Greece. Collectively they were responsible for sowing the seeds of Western civilization. Even when its influence waned, Athens remained a cultural mecca, a center for the study of philosophy and rhetoric, until the 6th century A.D. Throughout antiquity Athens was adorned with great public buildings, financed first by its citizens and later with gifts from Hellenistic kings and Roman emperors. Nowhere is the history of Athens so richly illustrated as in the Agora, the marketplace and focal point of life in the city.

A large open square surrounded on all four sides by public buildings, the Agora was in all respects the center of town. The excavation of buildings, monuments, and small objects has illustrated the important role it played in all aspects of civic life. The senate chamber *(bouleuterion),* public office buildings (Royal Stoa, South Stoa I), and archives *(metroon)* have all been excavated. The law courts are represented by the discovery of bronze ballots and a waterclock used to time speeches. The use of the area as a marketplace is suggested by the numerous shops and workrooms where potters, cobblers, bronzeworkers, and sculptors made and sold their wares. Long stoas, or colonnades, provided shaded walkways for those wishing to meet friends to discuss business, politics, or philosophy, and statues and commemorative monuments reminded citizens of former triumphs. A library and concert hall met cultural needs, and numerous shrines and temples in the area housed regular worship. Thus administrative, political, judicial, commercial, social, cultural, and religious activities all found a place here together in the heart of ancient Athens.

The many parts played by the Agora in the lives of the Athenians are reflected in the works of those ancient authors who frequented the Agora themselves. The heart of Athens was the scene of a mixture of political and commercial activity perhaps best described by the comic poet Euboulos:

You will find everything sold together in the same place at
Athens: figs, witnesses to summonses, bunches of grapes,
turnips, pears, apples, givers of evidence, roses, medlars,
porridge, honeycombs, chickpeas, lawsuits, first milk, pud-
dings, myrtle, allotment machines, irises, lambs, water-
clocks, laws, indictments. (Ath. 14.640b–c)

And for the Agora as a repository for reminders of former greatness,
Lykourgos comments:

You will find that in other cities statues of athletes are set
up in the agora, in Athens statues of good generals and of
the Tyrannicides. (Lykourg. *Leok.* 51)

Even those with no particular business to transact would find in the
Agora some entertainment to pass the time:

And yet at Athens lately, in front of the Painted Stoa, with
these two eyes I saw a conjuror devour a cavalry sword
sharpened to a very keen point; and presently, with the
inducement of a small payment, he also swallowed a
hunting spear, point first, till it penetrated deep into his
vitals. . . . And all of us who witnessed the performance
wondered. (Apul. *Met.* 1.4)

In its buildings and monuments the Agora came to be a cumulative
record of past achievement and history, and here the visitor to Athens
can recapture at least part of the richness and diversity of life in the
ancient city.

History
of the
Agora

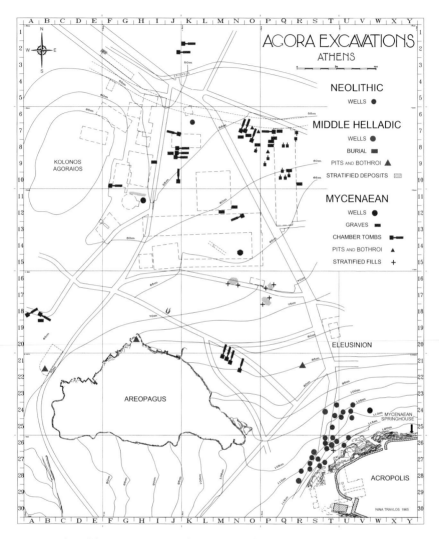

Figure 1. Plan of the Agora area in prehistoric times, showing Neolithic and Bronze Age wells and graves (3000–1100 B.C.)

THE EXCAVATIONS, WHICH COVER AN AREA of about 30 acres (12 hectares) northwest of the Acropolis, have brought to light remains from all periods of the city's history, from Neolithic times to the present, a span of some 5,000 years. On the slopes of the Acropolis, just below the Klepsydra spring, 20 shallow wells or pits of the Late Neolithic period (ca. 3000 B.C.) have been discovered (Fig. 1). The handmade pottery from these deposits is of excellent quality and shows that even at this remote period Athens had a settled population with high artistic standards. Scattered remains (wells and graves) of the Early and Middle Helladic periods (3000–1550 B.C.) have also been found.

The remains of the Late Helladic or Mycenaean period (1550–1100 B.C.) are more extensive. Two large chamber tombs, the first to be found in Athens, were located on the north slope of the Areopagus, and some 50 smaller tombs and simple graves of the same period were dotted throughout the area. A few household wells dating from the Late Mycenaean and the Submycenaean periods attest limited habitation in the level area as early as the 12th century B.C.

The Iron Age, comprising the Protogeometric and Geometric periods (1100–700 B.C.), is well represented (Fig. 2). More than 80 richly furnished graves have been found. No remains of houses have come to light, but 45 wells containing domestic refuse show that settlement was expanding in this direction.

Starting in the 6th century B.C., perhaps as early as the time of Solon the Lawgiver, the gently sloping area northwest of the Acropolis and east of Kolonos Agoraios may have been designated as the site of the main square of the city, the Agora, replacing an earlier center lying to the east of the Acropolis. Burials ceased to be made in this area and some private houses were demolished to make more open space for public needs.

During the half century (ca. 560–510 B.C.) when Athens was dominated politically by the tyrant Peisistratos and his family, the development of the Agora continued. A large houselike building dating from the early period of the tyrants preceded the Tholos at the southwest corner of the Agora; in later times it appears to have served the domestic needs of the Council, but it may have been built originally as a palace for the tyrants. A fountain house, supplied by a terracotta aqueduct, was built at the southeast corner of the square ㉒. The

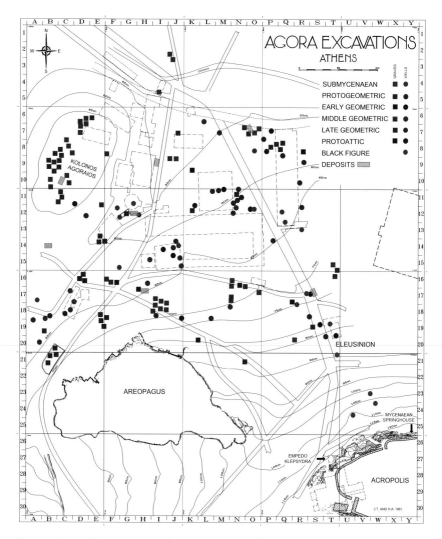

Figure 2. Plan of the Agora area, showing Iron Age and Early Archaic wells and graves (1100–600 B.C.)

grandson and namesake of Peisistratos established the Altar of the Twelve Gods **31**, and the family encouraged the development of the national festival of Athens, the Panathenaia, many events of which occurred in the Agora.

The increased tempo of civic life that followed the constitutional reforms of Kleisthenes at the end of the 6th century is reflected by building activity in the early years of the following century (Fig. 3). Many of the earliest substantial structures clearly designed for the needs of civic life seem to date to ca. 500 B.C. Boundary stones **10** now marked the limits of the open space. The southwest corner of the square was leveled and a great stone drain **11** was built to carry northward the surface water from the slopes of the Areopagus and from the valley between the Areopagus and the Pnyx. The small early buildings between this drain and Kolonos Agoraios were now demolished to

Figure 3. Plan of the Agora, ca. 500 B.C.

make way for the Old Bouleuterion (Council House) ⓮. A small temple to the north of and slightly later than the Old Bouleuterion may have housed the cult of the Mother of the Gods (the Temple of Meter). The Royal Stoa ㉖ also seems to date originally from the turn of the 6th to 5th century. The assembly of the citizens for political purposes *(ekklesia),* which had previously met in the Agora, now found a quieter meeting place on the Pnyx Hill, a 10-minute walk to the southwest (see Fig. 8). In keeping with this general trend toward more specialized facilities, many of the dramatic performances likewise gave up the Agora in favor of a more sheltered site at the south foot of the Acropolis.

The excavations have produced much evidence of the widespread damage done by the Persians who occupied Athens in 480/79 B.C. Private houses were destroyed and their wells filled with debris; sanctuaries such as those of Apollo and of the Twelve Gods were left desolate. The Aiakeion, the Old Bouleuterion, and the Royal Stoa presumably suffered as well but were subsequently repaired and continued in use.

To the 460s (i.e., the time of the Athenian statesman Kimon) are to be dated new civic buildings in the area of the Agora: the Tholos ❺, for the convenience of the Councillors, and the Painted Stoa, to serve as a pleasant promenade for the citizens. Kimon himself is reported to have adorned the Agora with plane trees.

Soon after the establishment of peace with the Persians in the mid-5th century B.C., the Athenians began to restore their ruinous sanctuaries. Among the first of the new buildings was the Temple of Hephaistos ❶. Work on the temple was interrupted, however, by the Periklean program on the Acropolis and was not resumed until the Peace of Nikias (421–415 B.C.). Other small sanctuaries and shrines were also repaired at this time (the Altar of the Twelve Gods, the Altar of Aphrodite). There was only limited civic building in the Agora during the Periklean period, the Strategeion(?), or headquarters of the generals ❼, being one of the few exceptions. As though to compensate for this neglect, a burst of activity followed in the last 30 years of the century (Fig. 4); the Stoa of Zeus ㉕, South Stoa I ㉔, the New Bouleuterion ⓭, and the Mint ㉛ all appear to date from this time even while Athens was engaged in the Peloponnesian War and its aftermath. Another civic improvement was the remodeling of the

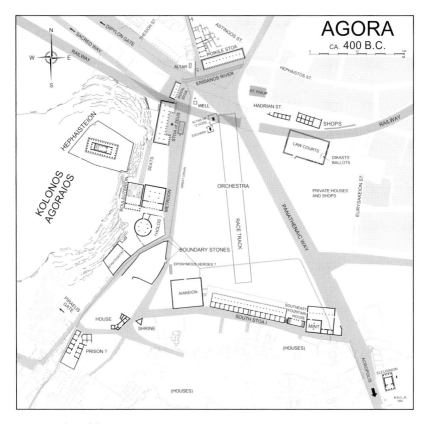

Figure 4. Plan of the Agora, ca. 400 B.C.

assembly place on the Pnyx at the end of the 5th century. With the disastrous loss of the Peloponnesian War, all public building projects ceased in the early 4th century B.C.

After a half century of no building activity, the second half of the 4th century saw a capacious new fountain house ⑳ erected at the southwest corner of the Agora and the Monument of the Eponymous Heroes ⑲ moved to a convenient location in front of the Old Bouleuterion. The period when Lykourgos controlled the city's finances (338–326 B.C.) witnessed many more improvements in the facilities for civic life (Fig. 5). The shrine of Zeus Phratrios and Athena Phratria was erected on the west side of the Agora ㉔, to be followed shortly by the construction of the Temple of Apollo Patroos ㉓. A group of buildings for the use of the law courts which had grown

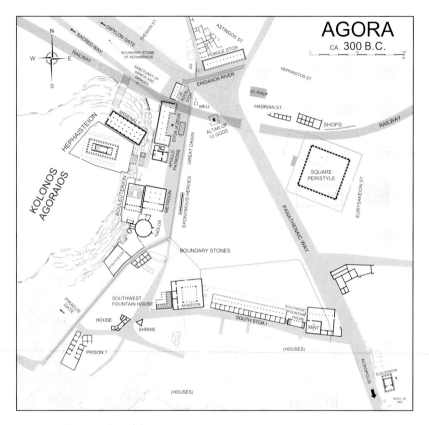

Figure 5. Plan of the Agora, ca. 300 B.C.

up at the northeast corner of the Agora in the later 5th and early 4th centuries B.C. was now replaced with a large cloisterlike building commonly referred to as the Square Peristyle **44**. Work on this structure was halted toward the close of the 4th century by the deteriorating military situation. This ushered in an unsettled period of more than a century during which little or no building occurred in the Agora.

   An improvement in the city's economy, combined with the benevolent attitude of the eastern monarchies, led to a renewal of building activity in the 2nd century B.C. (Fig. 6). The whole aspect of the Agora was changed in the course of the second and third quarters of the century by the erection of the Middle Stoa **67**, the East Building **66**, and South Stoa II **65**. The South Square thus formed took the place of several earlier buildings. The east side of the main square was now

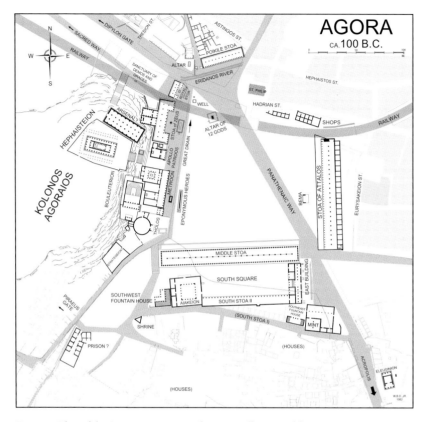

Figure 6. Plan of the Agora, ca. 100 B.C., showing Hellenistic additions

closed by a two-story colonnade **46**, the gift of Attalos II, King of
Pergamon (159–138 B.C.). The modernization was completed through
the construction of the Metroon on the west side of the square **14**.
This building replaced the Old Bouleuterion, which, after the construction of the New Bouleuterion late in the 5th century B.C., appears
to have housed both the state archives and a sanctuary of the Mother
of the Gods; the Hellenistic building served the same dual purpose.
This remodeling of the 2nd century B.C. fixed the main lines of the
Agora for the rest of antiquity. The area of the square and of the surrounding buildings was now about 50,000 square meters.

In 88 B.C. the Athenians espoused the cause of Mithradates VI,
king of Pontos, against Rome. After a long and bitter siege a Roman
army under Sulla broke through the western wall of the city on March

1, 86 B.C., and stormed into the area of the Agora. A great slaughter followed and many private houses were destroyed. A number of public buildings were damaged, among them the Tholos ❺, the Southwest Fountain House ❼⓿, the Aiakeion ❻❽, South Stoa II ❻❺, and the East Building ❻❻. The Tholos was soon repaired and, after a period of desolation, the south side of the Agora was reoccupied by private industrial establishments. These were built among the ruins of the old buildings, the remains attesting to marble workers, iron foundries, and potteries. Only in the time of Hadrian was this area cleaned up and restored to public use.

Meanwhile, and especially during the reign of Augustus, much had happened in the northern part of the Agora (Fig. 7). A concert hall, named after the donor as the Odeion of Agrippa, rose on the axis of the square ❹❶. The Temple of Ares, a building of the 5th century B.C., was transplanted from somewhere in Attica to the northwest corner of the Agora ❸❽ and the cult was apparently shared by Gaius Caesar, the adopted son of the emperor. At some time in the 1st century A.D. the Southwest and Southeast Temples, both made largely of reused material, were erected ❷⓿ ❺❷. An annex was built behind the Stoa of Zeus ❷❺ probably to receive an imperial cult, and the Civic Offices ❷❶ at the southwest corner of the square were designed to relieve pressure on the old administrative buildings. A columnar porch was added to the Tholos. Along the north side of the Agora, in its eastern part, a row of modest shops of the Classical period was now supplanted by a large building which is known as yet only by its deep Ionic porch facing south on the open square. With the aid of grants from Julius Caesar and the emperor Augustus, the Athenians were able to erect a splendid colonnaded marketplace 100 m to the east of the Classical-period Agora.

The 2nd century A.D. opened with the construction of a small public library near the southeast corner of the Agora; the building is known by the name of its founder, Titus Flavius Pantainos ❹❽. The construction of the Library was accompanied by the reorganization on a monumental scale of the roadway between the Classical-period Agora and the Market of Caesar and Augustus to the east ❹❼ (Fig. 8). Around the middle of the century a commercial building (the Southeast Stoa ❺❶) was erected on the east side of the Panathenaic Way to the south of the Library; its 11 shops were fronted by a deep Ionic porch, which was aligned with a similar porch on the Library to

Figure 7. Plan of the Agora in ca. A.D. 150, the period of greatest expansion and the time of the traveler Pausanias

create a street colonnade of a type much in vogue at that time. The appearance of the northeast corner of the square was also altered radically in the middle of the 2nd century by the construction of a basilica that presented its south end to the Agora **33**; the colonnade of the earlier building to the west was now extended around the end of the basilica. Among the last great architectural additions to this part of Athens was the library erected by the emperor Hadrian (A.D. 117–138) to the east of the Stoa of Attalos (see Fig. 8). The completion in A.D. 140 of an aqueduct begun by Hadrian permitted the erection of a semicircular fountain house *(nymphaion)* at the extreme southeast corner of the Agora **60**. Also to the Antonine period may be dated the construction of a charming round building in front of the Stoa

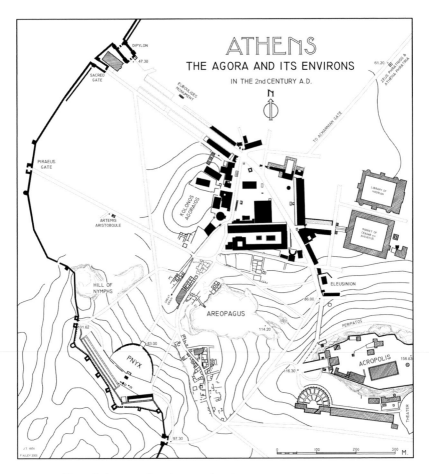

Figure 8. Agora and environs, 2nd century A.D.

of Attalos: the Monopteros **43**, built perhaps to shelter a statue. At about this time also occurred a radical reconstruction of the Odeion of Agrippa **41**.

In A.D. 267, the Herulians, a barbarian tribe from the north, invaded Greece. They sacked and burned several of the old cities including Athens. This raid was a turning point in the history of the city, the significance of which has been made clear for the first time by the Agora excavations. Most of the buildings in the region of the Agora, both public and private, were damaged. Public buildings elsewhere in the city and possibly even the temples on the Acropolis were burned.

Under the emperor Valerian (A.D. 253–260) and shortly before the raid, the outer defenses of the city were partially reconstructed on the line established by the 5th-century B.C. statesman Themistokles. But the outer circle could no longer be maintained, and so was temporarily abandoned. A much smaller inner circuit, which we shall refer to as the Post-Herulian Wall ❹❾, was now erected. It enclosed the Acropolis and the area immediately to the north, but not the Agora. This new wall was under construction during the reign of Probus (A.D. 276–282). It was built entirely of reused material, much of it from the shattered buildings of the Agora.

The one building which certainly survived the holocaust of A.D. 267 was the Temple of Hephaistos ❶, and evidence from the excavations now seems to show that several of the civic buildings on the west and north sides of the square, though perhaps damaged in A.D. 267, also continued to stand. Among these were the Tholos, the Temple of Apollo, the Stoa of Zeus, the Royal Stoa, and the Painted Stoa. During the 4th century the wall of the Tholos was strengthened, part of the Metroon seems to have been restored to use on a modest scale, and a good many of the large houses to the south and southwest of the Agora were reoccupied.

Disaster appears to have struck again toward the end of the 4th century A.D. The excavations indicate that the Tholos, the Temple of Apollo, the Stoa of Zeus, and the stoas bordering the road from the Dipylon Gate were destroyed at this time and abandoned. The probable culprit was Alaric at the head of a horde of Goths who appeared before the walls of Athens in A.D. 396. The literary evidence is divided regarding the damage done at this time to Athens and Attica, but the evidence of coins and pottery found in the debris overlying the floors of these buildings points to extensive destruction outside the walls in the closing years of the 4th century.

Yet even at this late date the city showed remarkable powers of recuperation (Fig. 9). Throughout the 4th century A.D. the philosophical schools of Athens had attracted scholars, both pupils and teachers, from far and near, and the fame of the schools continued through the following century. Already in the early years of the 5th century considerable building occurred in the area of the old Agora. Above the middle of the ancient square arose a huge new complex, the most conspicuous feature of which was the so-called Stoa of the Giants ❹❶.

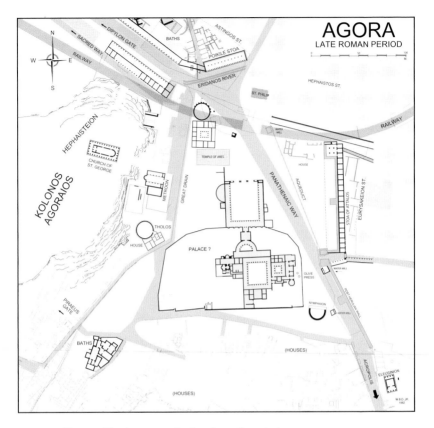

Figure 9. The Agora area in the 5th to 7th centuries A.D.

Also of early-5th-century date are a large square building with a colonnaded central court near the northwest corner of the Agora and, north of that, a round building of uncertain purpose. Toward the middle of the century colonnades were erected along the street bordering the north side of the area. In the same period a series of three water mills was installed along the east side of the Panathenaic Way in such a way that they were all turned in succession by the same water **50**.

The area suffered again from barbarian incursions in the 580s, and the continuing threat of further attacks led to the gradual abandonment of the area outside (i.e., to the west of) the Post-Herulian Wall. Within the shelter of that wall stratified deposits record the continuance of community life into the 8th century A.D., followed by a dark interval and then a general revival in the 10th century.

In later Byzantine, Frankish, and Ottoman times the area of the old Agora was chiefly a residential district. Excavators encountered large complexes of house foundations of the 11th and 12th centuries at a level high above the old classical floors. After being recorded they were removed to permit the study of earlier periods. Already by the early 7th century the ancient Temple of Hephaistos had been adapted to the needs of Christian worship. But the first church built as such within the area of the Agora dates from about A.D. 1000; it is the graceful little Church of the Holy Apostles that still stands above the southeast corner of the ancient square ⑥⑧. In 1204 the area suffered once more when much of the lower city was devastated by Leon Sgouros, dynast of Nauplion. The floors of the houses destroyed at this time were covered by a deep layer of silt pointing to several centuries of comparative desolation.

During the Greek War of Independence (A.D. 1821–1828), most of the houses then existing in the area were destroyed, particularly during the second siege of the Acropolis in 1827. One of these houses, situated a little to the southeast of the "Giants," belonged to the French consul Fr. S. Fauvel (1753–1838); some remnants of his large collection of antiquities were discovered when the area was excavated. After 1834, when Athens became the capital of the independent modern Greek state, the area was again developed as a residential district. The houses that were torn down to make way for the recent excavations were built for the most part about the middle of the 19th century (Fig. 10).

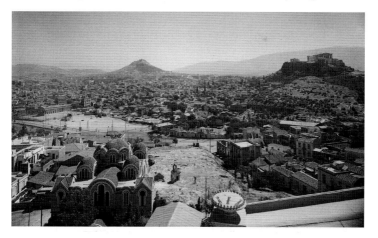

Figure 10. Area of the Agora, view looking east in 1930, before the excavations

History
of the
Excavations

IN 1832, IMMEDIATELY AFTER THE WAR OF INDEPENDENCE, two distinguished architects, S. Kleanthes and E. Schaubert, were commissioned by the Greek government to prepare a plan for the development of Athens as the capital of the new kingdom. They recommended that the new development be kept well to the north of the Acropolis so that "the area of the ancient cities of Theseus and of Hadrian" might be available for eventual exploration. Although this farsighted plan was upset by economic pressure, the Greek Archaeological Society took advantage of opportunities as they arose to explore individual monuments. Thus the Stoa of Attalos was cleared in a long series of campaigns (1859–1862, 1874, and 1898–1902). The Stoa of the Giants was opened up (1859, 1871, and 1912), and parts of the west side of the Agora were brought to light (1907–1908). On the west side the Greek archaeologists had taken over an area that was first excavated by the German Archaeological Institute in the years 1896–1897 as part of an extensive program for the exploration of the Agora area. In 1890–1891 a deep trench cut through the north part of the area for the Athens–Piraeus Railway brought to light remains of ancient buildings and sculpture; measured sketches were made by German archaeologists.

The great influx of refugees from Asia Minor after 1922 compelled the Greek state to consider the alternatives of proceeding with large-scale excavation or of relaxing restrictions and permitting the redevelopment of the area. With the financial backing of the late John D. Rockefeller Jr., the American School of Classical Studies was able to propose excavation. The Greek parliament passed legislation under which the School, having compensated the property owners, was entitled to excavate the area and to publish the results; on completion of excavation the area was to be landscaped. In accordance with existing Greek law, antiquities found by the excavators were to remain in Greece as the property of the Greek state. At this time the area was almost entirely covered by modern houses, more than 300 in number, which sheltered some 5,000 persons. Excavation began on May 25, 1931, and was continued in annual campaigns of four or five months each year through 1940 (Fig. 11). Before the outbreak of World War II, most of the area had been opened up and the outline of the ancient square had been established. After the war, fieldwork was resumed with the object of clearing the whole area down to the level

Figure 11. (top) The first day of excavations, May 25, 1931, looking west, with the Temple of Hephaistos in the background; (bottom) the same area showing the progress made nearly a month later.

of classical antiquity. This second series of campaigns extended from 1946 through 1960, by which time all the major buildings within the area had been explored, and numerous soundings had been made in the deeper levels.

The original concession had permitted the exploration of most of the west side of the Agora and the whole of both the east and the south sides. The north side of the ancient square was still to be found. It obviously lay to the north of the Athens–Piraeus Railway, which originally had been accepted as the northern limit. The search for the north side was begun in 1969 with the cooperation of the Greek state and with the financial support of the Ford Foundation and the Rockefeller Brothers Fund. The excavations in this area brought to light the Royal Stoa ㉖ at the extreme northwest corner of the square and a large basilica ㉝ at its northeast corner. New excavations, supported by the David and Lucile Packard Foundation, began in 1980 along the north side of Hadrian Street and have brought to light the sanctuary of Aphrodite ㉟ and the Stoa Poikile ㉟ along the north of the Agora square. Excavations in this area are expected to take several more years and are presently supported by the Packard Humanities Institute.

As the historical and architectural development of the Agora of Classical times became clearer, the problem of the relationship between the old square and the great Roman buildings to the east, namely the Market of Caesar and Augustus and the Library of Hadrian, became increasingly intriguing. Here again, thanks to the collaboration of the Greek state in making available the necessary property, excavation on a significant scale was carried out from 1971 to 1976.

As the excavation of the original concession neared an end, conservation and landscaping were undertaken. Many of the early and less substantial foundations were reburied after recording. Exposed foundations were reinforced where necessary for their preservation. Open areas among the buildings were leveled, and paths were laid out for the convenience of visitors. Trees and shrubs were planted, partly to beautify the area, partly to remind the visitor of an essential though seldom remembered element in the ancient setting. In the years 1953–1956, thanks again to the generous support of the late John D. Rockefeller Jr., the Stoa of Attalos, which had closed the east side of the square, was reconstructed to house the finds from the excavation and to provide a base of operations for further archaeological work in the area. In June 1957 the Greek Archaeological Service assumed responsibility for maintaining and guarding the archaeological area and the Stoa of Attalos. The American School retains working facilities in the stoa, and here are kept all the records of the excavation. Since 2000, in partnership with the Packard Humanities Institute, a project to computerize the entire excavation archive has been under way, some of the results of which can be seen at http://www.ascsa .edu.gr/agora.

📖

E. Capps, *Hesperia* 2 (1933), pp. 89–95; *Agora* XIV (1972), pp. 220–224; C. A. Mauzy, *Agora Excavations, 1931–2006: A Pictorial History* (Athens, 2006).

Tour
of the
Site

IDENTIFICATION

The location of the Agora in the area to the northwest of the Acropolis had been hesitantly inferred from references in the ancient authors; it was confirmed in 1938 by the discovery of a boundary marker of the Agora in its original position along the west side of the square **⑩**.

The identification of several of the individual monuments is made certain by inscriptions: the Sanctuary of the Twelve Gods **㉛**, the Stoa of Attalos **㊻**, and the Library of Pantainos **㊽**. The Tholos **⑤** was at once recognized from its round shape and early date; the Odeion of Agrippa **㊶** is the only theatrical building in an area where the existence of an odeion (music hall) is testified by the ancient authors.

The only ancient detailed description of the Agora that has come down to us occurs in the first book of Pausanias's *Description of Greece,* written about the middle of the 2nd century A.D., when the Agora was near the height of its development. Pausanias, proceeding from the Dipylon Gate, entered the square at its northwest corner and described many of the buildings and monuments. He was particularly interested in monuments that had religious and mythological associations, and in general he preferred the old to the new.

ROUTE

⓿ The archaeological area may be entered through any of three gates, one in the north side, one in the west side, and one at the southeast corner of the square. The southeast gate, near the Church of the Holy Apostles, is convenient for those approaching on foot from the Acropolis. Those coming on foot from the middle of the modern city may enter through the north gate near St. Philip's Church. The third entrance is to be found near the Temple of Hephaistos, whose other name, the "Theseion," is reflected in the nearby train station. An excellent overall view of the site is to be had either from the railway bridge inside the north gate or from the east end of the Temple of Hephaistos.

A site plan, with the individual buildings numbered, is in a pocket at the back of the book and cross-referenced in the text as **⓿**.

❶ TEMPLE OF HEPHAISTOS

Crowning Kolonos Agoraios, the Market Hill, is the Temple of Hephaistos, with which Athena was also associated; the two gods were
worshipped here by the Athenians as patron divinities of the arts
and crafts (Fig. 12). The identification is based chiefly on Pausanias's
account, reinforced by what is known from other authors and inscriptions about the cult statues and by the discovery around the temple
of much evidence of metalworking. Other identifications that have
been proposed include Theseus (hence the popular name "Theseion")
and Artemis Eukleia. Construction of the temple seems to have been
begun near the middle of the 5th century B.C.

A Doric peristyle surrounds a *cella* (main room) with *pronaos*
(antechamber) and *opisthodomos* (back room), each of which has its
own inner porch of two columns. The bottom step is of poros; above
this level all was of white marble: Pentelic for the building, Parian for
the sculpture. The style of the outside is clearly earlier than that of the
Parthenon, but there is reason to believe that the architect inserted an
interior colonnade within the cella as a result of seeing the designs
by Iktinos for the Parthenon, the construction of which was begun
in 447 B.C. The name of the architect of the Temple of Hephaistos
is unknown.

*Figure 12. The Hephaisteion: temple of Hephaistos, god of the forge, and Athena,
goddess of arts and crafts. Doric order, Pentelic marble, mid-5th century B.C.,
seen from the south.*

Figure 13. Conjectural restoration of the interior of the Hephaisteion

Bronze cult statues of Hephaistos and Athena were made by Alkamenes between the years 421 and 415 B.C.; these have perished (Fig. 13). The sculptures that remain on the outside of the building are of particular interest. Emphasis was placed on the ends of the temple, especially on the east front, which was quite prominent from the marketplace. Of the metopes (square panels in the frieze), only those above the east porch are carved. The ten on the east front illustrate nine of the labors of Herakles; from left to right, they show the Nemean Lion, the Hydra of Lerna, the Hind of Keryneia, the Boar of Erymanthos, the Mares of Diomedes, Kerberos, the Queen of the Amazons, Geryon (two metopes), and the Golden Apples of the Hesperides. Four of the labors of Theseus are represented on the north flank; from right to left appear the Sow of Krommyon, Skiron, Kerkyron, and Prokrustes. Another four on the south side show, from left to right, Periphetes, Sinis, the Bull of Marathon, and the Minotaur (Fig. 14). Because of their prominence, the Theseus metopes suggested the name "Theseion" for the temple in modern times. A ninth labor of Theseus was depicted on the continuous frieze above the inner porch of the pronaos. This frieze completed the rectangle, the other three sides of which were adorned with the sculptured metopes. The theme of the inner frieze is identified as the battle between Theseus and the sons of Pallas, his rivals for the throne, in the presence of six divinities, seated three on either side: Athena, Hera, and Zeus on the left; Hephaistos, Hippodameia, and Poseidon on the right. In the middle Theseus battles against his stone-throwing enemies. A corresponding frieze above the porch of the opisthodomos at the other end of the temple represents the battle between the Lapiths and the Centaurs. In the middle of the frieze

Theseus is again prominent as he rushes to the aid of the Lapith Kaineus, who is being hammered into the ground by two Centaurs (Fig. 15).

Shallow sockets in the floors of the triangular gable spaces at the ends of the temple attest to the existence of groups of pedimental sculpture. A few fragments of sculpture that have been found in the environs of the temple, and that are suitable in scale, quality, and date, may be attributed to these groups. All are of Parian marble, like the metopes and the inner friezes. The best preserved of the pedimental pieces is a group of one woman supporting another on

Figure 14. Theseus and Minotaur, southeast corner of the Hephaisteion

her back ⓜ; this was found in a well on the slope of the hill to the east of the temple. A torso of a thinly clad female figure, though found

Figure 15. Centaurs versus Kaineus, west frieze of Hephaisteion

Figure 16. Planting pits along south side of Hephaisteion, Hellenistic and Early Roman periods, at the time of excavation

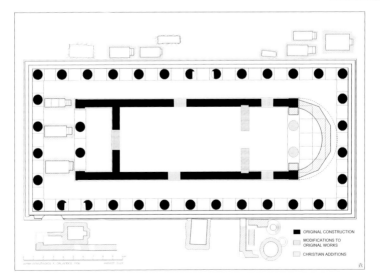

Figure 17. Plan of the Hephaisteion as the Church of St. George

on the floor of the Agora some 90 m to the east, may be an akroterion from the building .

The excavations produced evidence of a formal garden around the temple in Hellenistic and Early Roman times (Fig. 16). Rows of rectangular pits bordering the south, north, and west sides of the building contained flowerpots for the setting out of shrubs or small trees. The garden has been replanted with pomegranates next to the temple and myrtle in the outer rows. The flowerpots are in the Museum storerooms.

Having survived the disasters both of a.d. 267 and of the end of the 4th century, the temple was converted into a Church of St. George, probably in the 7th century A.D. (Fig. 17). The entrance was shifted from the east to the west end, two smaller doorways were opened in each of the side walls, the pronaos was replaced by an apse, and a barrel vault was erected over the cella. Many burials were made below the floors in the later Byzantine and Ottoman periods, and a number of distinguished Protestant visitors who died in Athens in the 18th and early 19th centuries were buried within the building. The cover stone from one of these graves, that of George Watson (died 1810), has been set against the inner face of the north wall; it bears an epigram in Latin by Lord Byron.

At the beginning of December 1834, King Otho entered Athens, the newly established capital of his kingdom; he was greeted by the local clergy with a Te Deum in the Church of St. George. This was the last occasion on which the building was used as a church. Thereafter it served as a local museum until the excavation of the 1930s.

General: *Hesperia* Suppl. 5 (1941); H. Koch, *Studien zum Theseustempel in Athen* (Berlin, 1955); J. Travlos, *Pictorial Dictionary of Ancient Athens* (London, 1971), pp. 261–273; *Agora* XIV (1972), pp. 140–149.

Cult images and pedestal: S. Karouzou, *AM* 69–70 (1954–1955), pp. 68–94; E. B. Harrison, *AJA* 81 (1977), pp. 137–178.

Sculpture: C. Morgan, *Hesperia* 31 (1962), pp. 210–235; H. A. Thompson, *AJA* 66 (1962), pp. 339–347; C. Morgan, *Hesperia* 32 (1963), pp. 91–108; A. Delivorrias, *Attische Giebelskulpturen und Akrotere des fünften Jahrhunderts* (Tübingen, 1974), pp. 16–60.

Roof and ceiling: W. B. Dinsmoor Jr., *AJA* 80 (1976), pp. 223–246; C. N. Edmonson and W. Wyatt, *AJA* 88 (1984), pp. 135–167.

Garden: D. B. Thompson, *Hesperia* 6 (1937), pp. 396–425.

Conversion to Christian use: A. Frantz, *DOP* 19 (1965), pp. 202–205.

❷ ❸ BUILDINGS NORTH OF THE TEMPLE OF HEPHAISTOS

North of the Temple of Hephaistos are remains of a number of buildings not sufficiently preserved to allow certain identification or detailed restoration (Fig. 18). The first of these, of which only a few foundation cuttings and blocks are now visible, was a large structure of the early 3rd century B.C. with buttressed walls; the interior was divided into three aisles. Water from the roof was carried under the foundations into cisterns at the southwest corner and near the middle of the north side of the interior. The massive construction of the building and its proximity to the city administrative buildings, to the Temple of Hephaistos, and to the quarter of the metalworkers suggest that it may have been a state arsenal ❷.

At the north foot of Kolonos Agoraios the construction of the Athens–Piraeus Railway brought to light and then obliterated a modest outdoor sanctuary of the People *(Demos)* and the Graces *(Charites)* ❸. A large marble altar which was found in place now stands in the National Museum; it bears a dedication of the year 197/6 B.C. to "Aphrodite, Leader of the People, and to the Graces." From other inscriptions it is known that the goddess Roma was also worshipped in this sanctuary.

From literary references we know that the sanctuary of the Salaminian hero Eurysakes, son of Ajax, was on Kolonos Agoraios. At this sanctuary gathered workmen waiting to be hired. Several inscriptions which stood in the sanctuary have come to light southwest of the Temple of Hephaistos, but no structural remains have yet been found.

📖

Arsenal: *Agora* XIV (1972), pp. 80–81; R. Pounder, *Hesperia* 52 (1983), pp. 233–256.

Demos and the Graces: *Agora* III (1957; reprinted 1973), nos. 125–132; J. Travlos, *Pictorial Dictionary of Ancient Athens* (London, 1971), pp. 79–81; *Agora* XIV (1972), p. 223.

Eurysakeion: W. S. Ferguson, *Hesperia* 7 (1938), pp. 1–74; *Agora* III (1957; reprinted 1973), nos. 246–255.

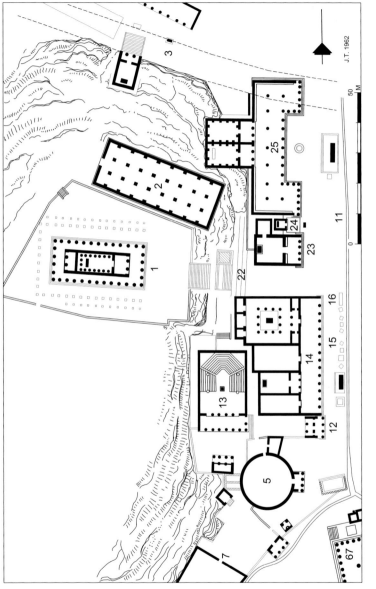

Figure 18. Buildings along the west side of the Agora. 2 = Arsenal (3rd century B.C.); 3 = Altar of Demos and Graces (2nd century B.C., now in National Museum).

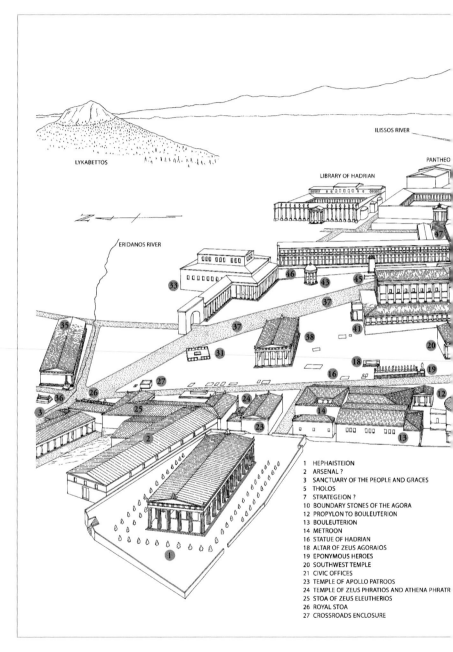

LYKABETTOS

ILISSOS RIVER

PANTHEO

LIBRARY OF HADRIAN

ERIDANOS RIVER

1 HEPHAISTEION
2 ARSENAL ?
3 SANCTUARY OF THE PEOPLE AND GRACES
5 THOLOS
7 STRATEGEION ?
10 BOUNDARY STONES OF THE AGORA
12 PROPYLON TO BOULEUTERION
13 BOULEUTERION
14 METROON
16 STATUE OF HADRIAN
18 ALTAR OF ZEUS AGORAIOS
19 EPONYMOUS HEROES
20 SOUTHWEST TEMPLE
21 CIVIC OFFICES
23 TEMPLE OF APOLLO PATROOS
24 TEMPLE OF ZEUS PHRATIOS AND ATHENA PHRATR
25 STOA OF ZEUS ELEUTHERIOS
26 ROYAL STOA
27 CROSSROADS ENCLOSURE

Figure 19. Restored perspective view of the Agora and environs in ca. A.D. 150, looking east

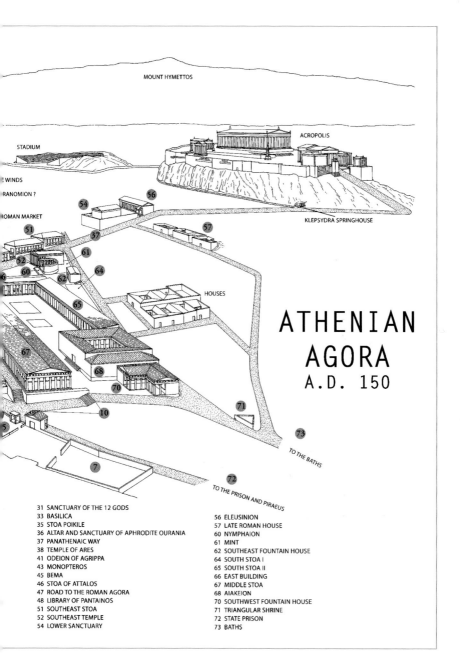

MOUNT HYMETTOS

ACROPOLIS

STADIUM

WINDS

RANOMION ?

ROMAN MARKET

KLEPSYDRA SPRINGHOUSE

HOUSES

ATHENIAN AGORA
A.D. 150

TO THE BATHS

TO THE PRISON AND PIRAEUS

31 SANCTUARY OF THE 12 GODS
33 BASILICA
35 STOA POIKILE
36 ALTAR AND SANCTUARY OF APHRODITE OURANIA
37 PANATHENAIC WAY
38 TEMPLE OF ARES
41 ODEION OF AGRIPPA
43 MONOPTEROS
45 BEMA
46 STOA OF ATTALOS
47 ROAD TO THE ROMAN AGORA
48 LIBRARY OF PANTAINOS
51 SOUTHEAST STOA
52 SOUTHEAST TEMPLE
54 LOWER SANCTUARY

56 ELEUSINION
57 LATE ROMAN HOUSE
60 NYMPHAION
61 MINT
62 SOUTHEAST FOUNTAIN HOUSE
64 SOUTH STOA I
65 SOUTH STOA II
66 EAST BUILDING
67 MIDDLE STOA
68 AIAKEION
70 SOUTHWEST FOUNTAIN HOUSE
71 TRIANGULAR SHRINE
72 STATE PRISON
73 BATHS

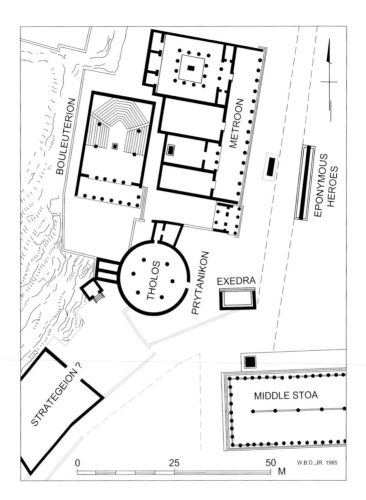

❹ BELVEDERE

Following the path southward from the east end of the Temple of
Hephaistos we come to a modern belvedere on the brow of the hill.
On the pedestal of the marble lectern is inscribed the name of Edward
Capps (1866–1955), who as chairman of the Managing Committee of
the American School of Classical Studies was in large part responsible
for the initiation of the Agora excavations. On top of the lectern is
a restored view of the Agora and environs as they appeared from
this spot (Fig. 19). Immediately in front of us at the foot of the hill
lie the ruins of the principal administrative buildings of the ancient
city (Fig. 20).

Figure 20. The Tholos-Bouleuterion complex: (facing page) plan and (above) aerial photograph

🔹 We continue down the path and recognize on our left the round floor of the Tholos.

⑤ THOLOS

In the *Constitution of the Athenians,* Aristotle writes:

> *Those members of the Council (boule) who are acting as chairmen (prytaneis) first eat together in the Tholos, receiving pay from the city; they next arrange the meetings of the Council and the Assembly.* (Arist. *Ath. Pol.* 43.3)

Other sources that dwell not so much on function as on shape make possible the identification of this round building as the Tholos, erected about 465 B.C. to replace an earlier structure.

Remains of the first period of the Tholos proper comprise only a few wall blocks of poros at the west (two courses), north, and southeast. The rest of the outer wall has been restored in dry masonry to the level of its latest floor in order to help conserve the building. In its original form the Tholos had no porch. Its floor was of hard-packed clay and lay at a level 45 cm below the present floor. There were six interior columns, the stumps of three of which are visible in the western half of the building; they are of poros and unfluted. Roof tiles belonging to this period were recovered. In the time of Augustus the porch was added, and soon afterward a pavement of marble chips was put in, still visible at a number of points.

The Tholos underwent an extensive remodeling, probably in the 2nd century A.D. The inner columns were cut down and the building was domed. The floor was paved with marble slabs bedded in mortar and the walls were revetted with marble. Subsequently, the wall was strengthened by a ring of concrete; this may have been necessitated by damage done in the Herulian sack. The building was finally abandoned about A.D. 400, presumably a consequence of the widespread destruction at that time. In the earlier periods of the Tholos a small room was attached to its north side; only a few blocks, belonging to various periods, are preserved. This was probably the kitchen. To the southeast of the Tholos, but within its precinct, are the massive foundations for a fountain fed by a pressure water pipe.

It was in the Tholos that the Athenian government had its headquarters. Here a number of the chairmen slept at night so that there were always responsible officials on hand. A set of standard weights and measures was kept here ⓜ. The building was the heart of the city administration and the seat of various cults connected with civic life. A marble inscription of about A.D. 200 found beside the building records

Figure 21. Model of the Tholos, showing one possible restoration of the roof of diamond-shaped tiles

Figure 22. A watercolor by Piet de Jong of the painted eaves tiles and a decorative antefix from the edge of the Tholos roof (ca. 465 B.C.)

the dedication of certain plants to the Phosphoroi, minor goddesses known to have been worshipped in the Tholos. Problems of interpretation remain as to how to roof the Tholos (unusual diamond-shaped tiles have been recovered), as well as how to restore accommodations

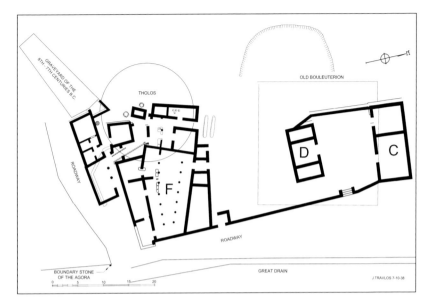

Figure 23. Early buildings along the west side: building F, mid-6th century B.C.; building C, early 6th century B.C.

for 50 or so diners in the building (Figs. 21, 22). A bench rather than couches seems to be the best solution for the dining issue.

The predecessor of the Tholos, building F (Fig. 23), was destroyed by the Persians in 480/79 B.C. Built in the mid-6th century B.C., it is made up of a colonnaded court surrounded by rooms of various shapes and sizes and looks in plan like a large-scale house. Originally it may have served the Peisistratid tyrants as a palace; following their expulsion it was presumably used as an official dining hall, as was its successor, the Tholos. At the northwest corner of the Archaic building was a long broiling pit, clearly designed to meet the needs of a large company. The rubble stonework foundations have been largely covered over again to assure their preservation; their tops project above the ground to the south of the Tholos.

📖

Tholos: E. Vanderpool, *Hesperia* 4 (1935), pp. 470–475; *Hesperia* Suppl. 4 (1940); *Agora* III (1957; reprinted 1973), nos. 589–609; J. Travlos, *Pictorial Dictionary of Ancient Athens* (London, 1971), pp. 553–561; J. McK. Camp II, *The Athenian Agora* (London, 1986), pp. 76–77, 94–97. **Building F**: T. L. Shear Jr., in *Athens Comes of Age* (Princeton, 1978), pp. 5–7.

➏ EARLY CEMETERY SOUTH OF THE THOLOS

At a still deeper level to the south of the Tholos was encountered a family burial plot containing 22 graves of the 8th, 7th, and early 6th centuries B.C. The area of the old graveyard was not built over in later times; it was enclosed and appears to have been regarded as a sacred place. In the Early Roman period the enclosure was adorned with a columnar gateway set in its south side, an arrangement commonly found in the sanctuaries of heroes *(heroa)*. The four-columned porch was put together of Doric elements reused from some earlier building. On the steep hill slope at the northwest corner of the enclosure are the foundation beddings for a small rectangular structure, perhaps a shrine, approached by a short flight of steps. To the left of the ancient steps and to the right of the modern is a marble base for some dedication.

📖

Early cemetery: *Hesperia* Suppl. 2 (1939).

➐➑ ADMINISTRATIVE BUILDINGS SOUTH OF THE THOLOS

Since the Tholos was the pivot about which the administration of the city-state revolved, facilities for various departments of the administration were naturally placed nearby. The principal buildings serving this purpose were the meeting place of the Council and the record office; these stood to the north of the Tholos. But other more modest buildings that have come to light to the south and southwest of the Tholos may be recognized as the offices of other administrative bodies. The Athenians called such buildings *archeia,* that is, the headquarters of various administrative boards *(archai).*

One such building ➐ stood to the southwest of the Tholos, from which it was separated by the sacred area above the ancient cemetery. The structure was set in a deep cutting in the slope of the hill. The trapezoidal plan comprised a central courtyard bordered by seven or eight rooms; a cistern with two mouths lay beneath the court. The construction dates from soon after the middle of the 5th century B.C., but beneath the floors of the period have been noted foundations of an earlier structure, while the plan of the 5th-century building has been confused by various concrete foundations of Roman date.

The size and the prominent position of this building, as well as the great effort involved in leveling the site, suggest an important establishment. A possible candidate is the Strategeion, the headquarters of the 10 generals *(strategoi)*. In the Strategeion the military commanders transacted their business, dined, and sacrificed in common. Other identifications are possible. The discovery in 2005 of a hoard of some 383 Athenian silver coins, buried beneath the floor of one of the rooms, perhaps suggests that the *poletai* (state auctioneers), who were responsible for leasing out the state-owned silver mines at Laureion, were housed in the building. A number of inscriptions recording such leases have been found around the southwest corner of the Agora. Alternatively, the individual rooms may have been used for commercial purposes.

To the south of the Tholos, in the triangular space between the Great Drain and the west end of the Middle Stoa, are the scanty remains of a crowded group of small buildings ❽ dating chiefly from the 5th and 4th centuries B.C. Their outlines are more distinct in the site plan than on the ground. Three buildings may be distinguished; they stood on the north, west, and south sides of a courtyard with a well near its middle. The southern building comprised a single row of three rooms; the western consisted of eight rooms in two rows; the northern had one small and one large room, which shared a colonnade facing onto the court.

The plans of these buildings are less suitable to houses than to shops or offices. Their proximity to the Agora, and more specifically to the Tholos and Bouleuterion, suggests that they too were part of the public offices *(archeia)*. From a well of the late 5th century B.C. at the northern tip of the triangular area was recovered a *klepsydra* or waterclock of the type used for measuring speeches in the law courts ⓜ, and a number of bronze ballots used by members of the jury in recording their votes have also come to light within the triangular area. Such a concentration of material, rare within the excavated area, suggests that some law court met in the area or stored its equipment in one of the buildings. The most recent excavations indicate that by the 4th century B.C. at least some of these buildings served a commercial function.

Agora XIV (1972), pp. 72–74.

⑨ HOUSE OF SIMON THE COBBLER

The remains found in the north part of the triangular area, on the other hand, are of a more private nature (Fig. 24). The excavations revealed the foundations of a couple of rooms facing onto a courtyard in which was a well and a cesspool. In levels of the second half of the 5th century B.C. were found many large-headed iron hobnails of the sort used in the soles of heavy boots, as well as a group of bone eyelets for laces (Fig. 25). They were numerous enough to suggest the existence of a shoemaker's shop. The base of a drinking cup found in the same context bears the name of its owner, Simon. This may well have been the shoemaker of that name whose shop near the Agora is known to have been frequented by Sokrates:

> *Simon, an Athenian, a shoemaker. When Sokrates came*
> *to his workshop and discoursed, he used to make notes of*
> *what he remembered, whence these dialogues were called*
> *"The Shoemaker's."* (Diog. Laert. 2.13.122)

Figure 24. Ruins of the house of Simon the Cobbler, 5th century B.C.,
set up against an Agora boundary stone (center foreground)

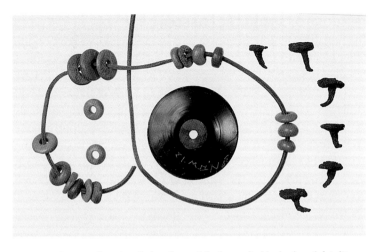

Figure 25. Bone eyelets, iron hobnails, and the base of a black-glazed drinking cup inscribed with the name Simon

All the buildings in the triangular area were demolished in the middle of the 2nd century B.C. to make way for the west end of the Middle Stoa. Their walls were stripped down to ground level, and the foundations were overlaid by the graveled surface of a roadway that jogged around the west end of the stoa, replacing an earlier north–south road that was overlaid by the stoa. Toward the southwest corner of the area, and convenient to the entrance to the Agora, a small public latrine was now built beside the west branch of the Great Drain. There are remnants of the deep plastered channels and of the characteristic flooring made from the chips of roof tile.

House of Simon: D. B. Thompson, *Archaeology* 13 (1960), pp. 234–240; *Agora* XIV (1972), pp. 173–174.

⑩ BOUNDARY STONES OF THE AGORA

While in this area we may pause over two small monuments of singular interest for the topography of the Agora. These are rectangular posts of Parian marble each inscribed in Attic lettering of about 500 B.C.: "I am the boundary of the Agora" (Fig. 26). (Both posts have been replaced by casts, but the originals are on display in the Museum Ⓜ.) One of these posts stood at the angle of a wall of the home of Simon the cobbler about 20 m to the east of the Tholos;

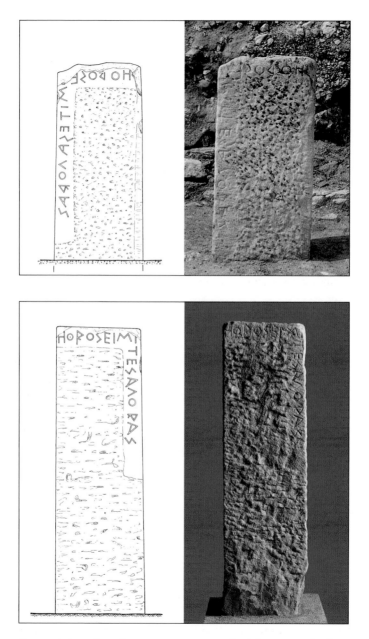

Figure 26. Agora boundary stones, ca. 500 B.C.: (top) the stone under the west end of the Middle Stoa (I 7039) (drawing and photo); (bottom) the stone southeast of the Tholos (I 5510) (drawing and photo)

the other was found deep inside the west end of the Middle Stoa, again rising beside an early wall. In each case the marker was placed in relation to a contemporary entrance to the Agora, and it is to be assumed that the other entrances to the square were similarly marked to emphasize the distinction between the Agora square proper and the many sacred and official precincts that bordered the open space. This formality was necessary because the Agora itself was a precinct from which certain types of criminals were barred by law and within which no private citizen was allowed to build.

Further evidence of the sacred nature of the Agora is to be seen at a higher level to the east of the first boundary stone. Here is the stump of a marble pedestal which supported a holy water basin (*perirrhanterion*) used for purification rites on entry into the Agora: "so the lawmaker keeps outside the perirrhanteria of the Agora the man who avoids military service, or plays the coward, or deserts" (Aeschin. 3.176). Two other such basins have been found in the excavations; although not found in situ, they probably come from other entrances to the square. The difference in level between the boundary stone to the east of the Tholos and the adjacent *perirrhanterion* illustrates the depth of accumulation between the 5th century B.C. and the 1st century A.D.

Agora III (1957; reprinted 1973), nos. 713, 714; Agora XIV (1972), pp. 117–119.

⓫ THE GREAT DRAIN AND ITS BRANCHES

Standing beside the first of the two boundary stones of the Agora, we look north into the main channel of the Great Drain.

The drainage of the Agora area together with the adjacent hill slopes was assured by a simple but effective system of stone-lined channels (Fig. 27). They were covered with loosely jointed stone slabs, the tops of which were flush with the graveled surface of the square. Although these great drains received a certain amount of sewage from nearby houses and shops, their primary function was to handle the torrents of surface water that descended into the square at times of heavy rain. It was the neglect of this drainage system in late antiquity that led to the silting of the area.

In the early years of the 5th century B.C. the main drainage channel was constructed on the west side of the area, presumably as part of

Figure 27. Great Drain, late 6th/early 5th century B.C.

a program to improve the setting for the early buildings erected in the Agora, such as the Old Bouleuterion ⓮ and the Aiakeion ㊽. Starting with a funnel-shaped open mouth at a point about 20 m to the east of the (later) Tholos, the new drain followed a very regular course almost due north to issue from the square through its northwest corner. Bearing westward at this point, it joined a still larger channel, the canalized form of the Eridanos River, to continue northwestward under the Panathenaic Way and eventually to pass through the city wall alongside the Sacred Gate.

The original construction of the drain may best be studied to the east of the Metroon. Here the channel measures 1 m in both width and depth. The walls are of hard breccia beautifully jointed in polygonal style; the floor is paved with limestone. Most of the original cover slabs of soft yellowish limestone have been replaced through the ages with miscellaneous material including gravestones, inscriptions, and even statues. Farther north, opposite the Stoa of Zeus and the Royal Stoa, the channel becomes much deeper and is built of soft poros in ashlar masonry; this represents a rebuilding in the 4th century B.C.

At the turn of the 5th–4th century B.C. the single line of drain was supplemented by two feeders, one coming from the southeast and the other from the southwest, to join the original channel in a Y-shaped formation at a point opposite the Tholos. The eastern branch had its beginnings high in the gully between the Acropolis and Areopagus. Thence it descended on a northwesterly course, probably following an earlier line of the Panathenaic Way, to a point beneath the east end of the (later) Middle Stoa **67**. Here it bent sharply westward to join the main stem. The western branch drained the valley between the Areopagus and Pnyx and entered the Agora on a northeasterly course in the bottom of the valley between the Areopagus and Kolonos Agoraios. Both branches in their lower parts were comparable in dimensions with the main channel; they were built of soft poros in regular masonry.

The whole of this ancient drainage system, having been cleared and reconditioned by the excavators, again functions perfectly and keeps the entire area dry.

Drains: *AgPicBk* 11 (1968); *Agora* XIV (1972), pp. 194–197.

✷ We now resume our examination of the administrative buildings, moving on to those that stood north of the Tholos.

⑫ GATEWAY TO THE NEW BOULEUTERION

Access to the New Bouleuterion **⑬**, the meeting place of the Council, was through a roofed gateway *(propylon)* of the Ionic order **⑫**, the foundations of which are to be seen just south of the Metroon **⑭**. This gateway, along with the passage that led back to the New Bouleuterion and the porch at the south end of the New Bouleuterion, all appear to be of the second half of the 4th century B.C. In front of the Propylon are traces of a fountain.

⑬ NEW BOULEUTERION

The New Bouleuterion (Council House) occupied a terrace cut back into the hillside northwest of the Tholos. It was built at the end of the 5th century B.C., apparently to take over the function of its eastern neighbor, the Old Bouleuterion. It was in the Bouleuterion that members of the Council of 500 *(boule)* held the meetings in which they did committee work and prepared legislation for the Assembly. The Council, made up of 50 citizens from each of the 10 tribes, was chosen by allotment each year, and these tribal contingents of 50 served in rotation as group chairmen *(prytaneis)* of the Council.

The outline of the New Bouleuterion may be seen in the cuttings for its foundation walls, some blocks of which remain. It seems clear that the auditorium faced south, though little evidence for the original seating arrangements survives. The condition of the dressed bedrock within the area suggests, however, that in the beginning the seats were of wood and supported on wooden beams. A number of curved marble floor slabs found within the building and now lying along its west side indicate that at some later date curved seating of stone was installed (Fig. 28).

Two large bottle-shaped cisterns, cut in the rock just west of the building, gathered rainwater from its roof. They are joined by a tunnel with a cistern to the southwest of the Tholos, which probably took its water from the roof of that building. This capacious reservoir was no doubt intended primarily to meet the housekeeping needs of the Tholos.

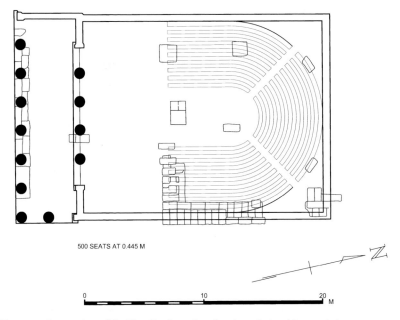

500 SEATS AT 0.445 M

0   10   20
                          M

Figure 28. Restoration of the New Bouleuterion showing relationship to existing foundation, late 5th century B.C. The auditorium seems to have faced south, though the restoration of the seating, curved or rectilinear, is uncertain.

⑭ METROON AND OLD BOULEUTERION

The Metroon, built in the mid-2nd century B.C., consists of four rooms of various sizes sharing a colonnade that faces eastward toward the square. Three steps of Hymettian marble and an Ionic column base of Pentelic marble are preserved toward the south end of the colonnade. In the line of the north wall a pair of orthostates (upright wall blocks) remain in position; elsewhere only the foundations are preserved (Fig. 29).

The building accommodated both the sanctuary of the Mother of the Gods *(Meter Theon),* from which it took its name, and the state archives. The second room from the south, which has the plan of a small temple, was probably the actual sanctuary of the goddess. If so, the heavy foundation in front of the building opposite this room may well have held the altar. The first and third rooms from the south presumably contained the actual state documents, written on papyrus and parchment. The large northern room had two stories around a central court with an altar at its middle. The function of this room is unknown, though it may have served as the reading room. Alternatively, the open court covers the early temple of the Mother and it may have housed her cult.

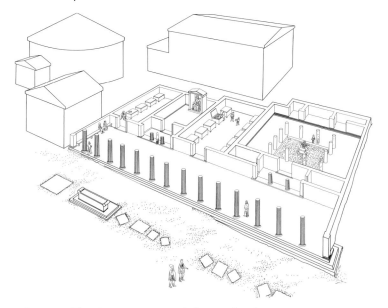

Figure 29. The Metroon in its second phase, mid-2nd century B.C.

The mosaic pavement in the third room from the south does not belong to the original building but dates from a partial reconstruction in the early 5th century A.D. It lies at a much lower level than the original floor of the building. In the same late period the northern room was rearranged in the form of a basilica. The purpose of the building in this late period is obscure, though a sculpted plaque with palm tree and menorah found in the area suggests the possible use of the room as a synagogue.

The area inside the Metroon has been excavated to bedrock, which lies in some places as much as 3 m below the top of the front foundation (now partially refilled). Remains of several earlier buildings have come to light.

Directly behind and partly underneath the foundation for the southern part of the Hellenistic colonnade is a massive foundation of Acropolis limestone. At the north, this foundation turns west at right angles and runs under the Hellenistic wall. The earlier building was square, 20 m on a side, and dates from early in the 5th century B.C. It has been identified as the Old Bouleuterion, perhaps built soon after the reforms of Kleisthenes to accommodate the newly formed Council of 500 (Figs. 30, 31). In addition to serving as a council house, the building sheltered the famous statue of the Mother of the Gods, a work attributed by some ancient sources to Pheidias and by others, with more probability, to his favorite pupil, Agorakritos (Fig. 32). Here too were stored various documents of public interest written on papyrus or parchment or whitened wooden tablets, and occasionally on marble. Toward the end of the 5th century, with the growing

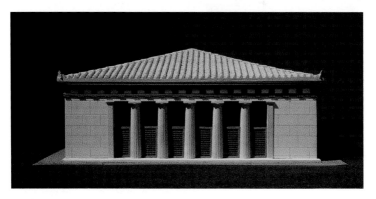

Figure 30. Model of the Old Bouleuterion, ca. 500 B.C.

Figure 31. Restored perspective drawing of the interior of the Old Bouleuterion, during a meeting, ca. 500 B.C.

complexity of administration, a more systematic procedure was introduced into the keeping of public records, and something like archives in the modern sense of the word began to take shape. It may indeed

Figure 32. Miniature copy of the statue of the Mother of the Gods, the original of which stood in the Metroon

have been the accompanying need for more space that led to the construction of the New Bouleuterion. We may assume that the meetings of the Council from then on took place in the new building while the old continued to be used as a sanctuary and as a repository of records.

Contemporary with the Old Bouleuterion, and oriented in relation to it, was a small Archaic temple presumably of the Mother of the Gods, some foundations of which may still be seen in the north room of the Metroon. This temple seems to have been destroyed by the Persians in 480/79 B.C. and was never rebuilt. But the name and function of the Metroon indicate that worship of the Mother continued in the area.

In the colonnade in front of the northern room of the Metroon is a foundation belonging to a smaller and still earlier building (building C). Within the northern room itself are other walls of the same building (see Fig. 23); this earlier structure dates from the early 6th century B.C. (i.e., from the time of Solon). It is not clear whether it should be regarded as a public or private building.

📖

Bouleuterion and Metroon: H. A. Thompson, *Hesperia* 6 (1937), pp. 115–127; *Agora* III (1957; reprinted 1973), nos. 387–433, 465–519; *Agora* XIV (1972), pp. 25–38.

⑮ MONUMENT BASES NEAR THE METROON
In front of the Metroon and around its northeast corner is a thickset row of monument bases, an indication of the prominence of this area. None of the individual monuments have been identified. The excavation showed that some of the bases had probably been stripped after the Roman siege of 86 B.C.

⑯ STATUE OF HADRIAN
Near the northeast corner of the Metroon has been set up a statue of the emperor Hadrian (A.D. 117–138). It was found in the early years of the excavation lying in the Great Drain a little to the east; the torso in fact had been reused in late antiquity as a cover slab for the drain. Despite the absence of a head, the identification as Hadrian is certain because of the decoration on the cuirass: Athena, flanked by her symbols, the owl and the serpent, and crowned by two Winged Victories, stands upon the wolf symbolizing Rome, which is suckling Romulus and Remus (Fig. 33). This is one of several such statues found in Greece, visual expressions of Roman appreciation and enthusiasm for the more sophisticated art and culture of the Greek world they now dominated. The sentiment of "captive taking the captor captive" (paraphrasing the Roman poet, Horace) is particularly suitable to the philhellene Hadrian, who visited Athens three times during his reign. This is perhaps the statue of Hadrian that Pausanias saw near the Stoa of Zeus (Paus. 1.3.2).

📖

T. L. Shear Jr., *Hesperia* 2 (1933), pp. 178–183.

Figure 33. Statue of the emperor Hadrian (A.D. 117–138) with cuirass showing Athena and the wolf of Rome

⑰ MONUMENT OF QUINTUS TREBELLIUS RUFUS

To the east of the Great Drain has been set up a large marble statue base reassembled from many fragments found in this area. The principal inscription on the face of the pedestal records a vote of thanks to Quintus Trebellius Rufus, a benefactor of the Athenians, who came from the city of Toulouse in Narbonese Gaul (France); included in the honors are his wife and son. Lower on the face of the stone are two letters addressed to the Athenian councils and people, written by the governing bodies of the province of Narbonese Gaul and Toulouse. The date is toward the end of the 1st century A.D., but the nature of Trebellius Rufus's benefactions is unknown.

Near the pedestal of Trebellius Rufus are several bedding blocks for bronze stelai triangular in section. These may be the stelai on which were engraved the lists of ephebes, the young men undergoing military training. Aristotle (Arist. *Ath. Pol.* 53.4) speaks of such a stele "in front of the Bouleuterion, beside the Eponymoi."

Q. Trebellius Rufus: J. H. Oliver, *Hesperia* 10 (1944), pp. 72–77. **Bronze stelai**: R. S. Stroud, *Hesperia* 32 (1963), p. 143.

⑱ ALTAR OF ZEUS AGORAIOS(?)

A little to the southeast of the Trebellius Rufus monument are the remains of a large altar of Pentelic marble (Fig. 34). From the style of the workmanship it can be dated to the late 4th century B.C. The presence of letters on the ends of the blocks, however, in a style current in the 1st centuries B.C. and A.D., can only mean that the altar was dismantled at that time and reerected in its present position. The letters were inscribed by masons so that the blocks could be correctly reassembled. A cutting for a monument of similar size has been found

Figure 34. Altar of Zeus Agoraios(?), 4th century B.C., moved into the Agora in Roman times

on the Pnyx, and it may well be that the altar originally stood there. The divinity to whom the altar was dedicated may have been Zeus Agoraios, the inspirer of oratory. This attribution best explains a scholiast's comment that "Zeus Agoraios is established in the Agora and in the Assembly Place."

The oak and laurel trees flanking the altar were planted in 1954 by King Paul and Queen Frederika to inaugurate the program of landscaping.

R. Stillwell, *Hesperia* 2 (1933), pp. 140–148; *Agora* III (1957; reprinted 1973), nos. 379–386; *Agora* XIV (1972), pp. 160–162.

⑲ MONUMENT OF THE EPONYMOUS HEROES

In front of the Metroon-Bouleuterion complex and to the east of the Great Drain are the remains of a long pedestal enclosed by a fence. From a reference in Pausanias (1.5) we know that the pedestal supported statues of the 10 legendary heroes of Attica who became the patrons of the 10 tribes *(phylai)* into which Kleisthenes, in 508 B.C., divided the population of Attica for administrative and political purposes. The original heroes as named by Pausanias were Hippothoon, Antiochos, Ajax, Leos, Erechtheus, Aigeus, Oineus, Akamas, Kekrops, and Pandion (Fig. 35). In 307/6 B.C. the number was increased by the addition of Antigonos and Demetrios, kings of Macedon, who were dropped from the list a century later when Athens and Macedon became embroiled in war. Ptolemy III Euergetes, king of Egypt, was added in 224/3 B.C.; Attalos I, king of Pergamon, in 200 B.C.; and

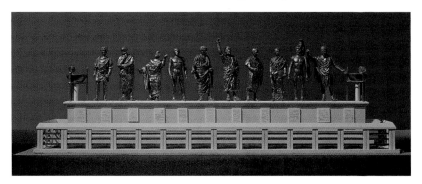

Figure 35. Model of the Monument of the Eponymous Heroes, second half of the 4th century B.C., before addition of new tribal heroes

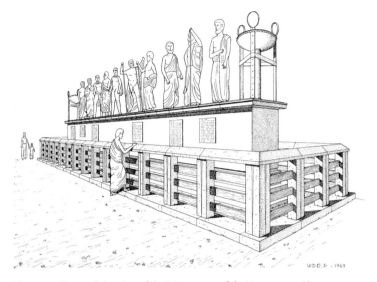

Figure 36. Restored drawing of the Monument of the Eponymous Heroes, second half of the 4th century B.C., before addition of new tribal heroes

Hadrian, emperor of Rome, about A.D. 125. A close study of the surviving blocks has revealed the ingenious ways in which provision was made for the fluctuating number of statues. The final addition, that of Hadrian, required a southward extension of pedestal and fence.

In addition to this honorary function, the monument served a practical purpose as the official notice board of the city. Here, for instance, were posted drafts of proposed new laws for consideration by the citizens, lists of men called up for military service, and notices of impending lawsuits (Fig. 36).

Enough remains to indicate the design of the monument. The high continuous pedestal was crowned by a marble course of which two blocks have survived. In the top of one are cuttings for the feet of a slightly more than life-size bronze statue. The other block, from one end of the pedestal, carried a large bronze tripod. The marble course projected far enough to protect the notices, which, as we know from the ancient authors, were written on whitened wooden boards and hung on the face of the pedestal. The fence consisted of stone posts and crowning member with wooden rails; in a reconstruction of the Roman period the stone was replaced by white marble on the east side.

The Monument of the Eponymous Heroes is mentioned by Aristophanes in the *Peace* (421 B.C.), but the architectural style and the ceramic evidence indicate a date after 350 B.C. for the existing monument, nor is there any trace of an earlier structure on this site. The original monument must have stood elsewhere, perhaps on a foundation that has come to light to the south, under the west end of the Middle Stoa.

Agora III (1957; reprinted 1973), nos. 229–245; T. L. Shear Jr., *Hesperia* 39 (1970), pp. 145–222; *Agora* XIV (1972), pp. 160–162.

⑳ SOUTHWEST TEMPLE

At some time after the construction of the Odeion ㊶, but before the erection of the Civic Offices ㉑, the angle between the Odeion and the Middle Stoa was occupied by a newly founded sanctuary. The temple consisted of a cella with a porch facing west (Fig. 37). Masonry has survived only at the southwest corner, consisting of heavy conglomerate blocks above a packing of broken stone set in crumbly lime mortar. Elsewhere the plan has been recovered only from beddings. The superstructure was built of reused material from a Doric building of Classical date that originally stood at Thorikos, in southeastern Attica. After the destruction of the Southwest Temple, the pieces were used again in the Late Roman fortification wall ㊾ (see Fig. 100).

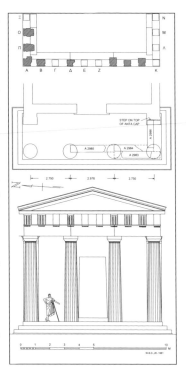

Figure 37. Restored plan and elevation of the Southwest Temple, showing reused Doric architecture

W. B. Dinsmoor Jr., *Hesperia* 51 (1982), pp. 410–466.

㉑ CIVIC OFFICES

The modest complex of buildings at the foot of the terrace of the Middle Stoa and to the west of the Odeion dates from the 2nd century A.D.

The principal building comprised three rooms diminishing in size from east to west in such a way as to interfere as little as possible with traffic through the southwest entrance to the Agora; a still smaller fourth room at the west end of the building was demolished in the interest of freer circulation.

The large east room had a northern porch. At the east and west sides of the room a low bench built of clay with plastered top and front stood against the wall. In the angle between the first and second rooms from the east stand a pair of marble slabs that were found

Figure 38. Tile standard, a marble model for terracotta roof tiles, found in the Civic Offices

nearby and have been set up on their original pedestal. These slabs have representations of roof tiles carved on their faces; they undoubtedly served as official standards (Fig. 38). This provision for the control of commerce is reminiscent of the weights and measures maintained in the Tholos and suggests that the building was designed to provide additional space for the public offices originally accommodated in the Tholos and Metroon. Its public character is further illustrated by the beddings for stelai in front of the second room from the east.

Between the Civic Offices and the Odeion are the remains of a small colonnade with a compartment at its east end corresponding to the east room of the Civic Offices. Nothing remains but the conglomerate foundations; their high level indicates that the builders of the stoa adjusted their ground level to that of the Southwest Temple.

Civic Offices, tile standard: G. P. Stevens, *Hesperia* 19 (1950), pp. 174–188; *Agora* XIV (1972), p. 79.

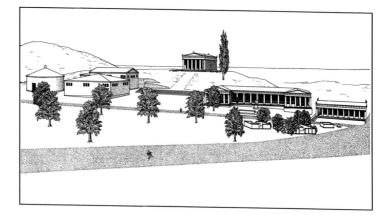

Figure 39. Buildings along the west side of the Agora in the 5th century B.C. From left to right: Tholos, Old Bouleuterion, New Bouleuterion (behind), Hephaisteion, Stoa of Zeus Eleutherios, and Royal Stoa. The stone benches are in the center, below the Hephaisteion.

㉒ BENCHES ON KOLONOS AGORAIOS

On the lower slope of the hill northwest of the Metroon are a few blocks of soft, gray poros, the remains of four rows of simple benches (Fig. 39). Dating from the second half of the 5th century B.C., they clearly served as a meeting place for one of the law courts or governing bodies of Athens. Such a meeting place, known as the *synedrion,* is known to have been in the vicinity.

H. A. Thompson, *Hesperia* 6 (1937), pp. 218–220; A. L. Boegehold, *Hesperia* 36 (1967), pp. 111–120.

㉓ TEMPLE OF APOLLO PATROOS

A small Ionic temple, with columns only at the east, is identified by Pausanias as the Temple of Apollo Patroos, who was worshipped by the Athenians as "Fatherly Apollo" because of the legend which made him the father of Ion, founder of the Ionian race of which the Athenians were a part (Fig. 40). In this capacity Apollo was one of the patron deities of the state organization, especially in connection with the brotherhoods (*phratries*); children of Athenian citizens were formally presented to fellow members of the brotherhood and to Apollo Patroos.

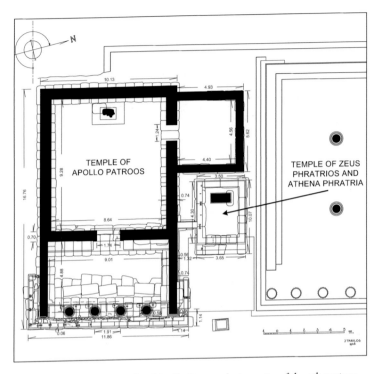

Figure 40. Plan of the Temple of Apollo Patroos, last quarter of the 4th century B.C., with the tiny Temple of Zeus Phratrios and Athena Phratria(?) to the north

According to Pausanias (1.3.4), the cult statue was by Euphranor, a leading Athenian artist of the 4th century B.C. Euphranor's work has been recognized in a colossal statue found near the temple by the Greek Archaeological Society in its 1907 excavations; it now stands in the Stoa of Attalos (Fig. 41). Other statues of Apollo by Leochares and Kalamis that are mentioned by Pausanias may have stood in the porch of the temple on a pedestal formed by a curious thickening of the front walls.

Opening off the north side of the main room, or cella, of the temple is a smaller room, certainly contemporary; this was presumably an adyton or inner sanctuary, a familiar feature in temples of Apollo. The temple seen by Pausanias dates from the last quarter of the 4th century B.C. Beneath the floor level of its cella are slight remains of an earlier building, possibly a temple. An arc of its curved west wall and a small square base of poros remain but have been covered over.

Figure 41. Apollo Patroos(?), perhaps by Euphranor, second half of the 4th century B.C.

In a casting pit a few meters to the south of the temple (no longer visible) was found a mold for the casting of a bronze statue, two-thirds life size, perhaps of Apollo 🅼, dating to the mid-6th century B.C.

H. A. Thompson, *Hesperia* 6 (1937), pp. 77–115; *Agora* III (1957; reprinted 1973), nos. 107–113; J. Travlos, *Pictorial Dictionary of Ancient Athens* (London, 1971), pp. 96–99; C. Hedrick, *AJA* 92 (1988), pp. 185–210; M. Lawall, *Hesperia* 78 (2009), p. 387.

㉔ TEMPLE OF ZEUS PHRATRIOS AND ATHENA PHRATRIA

Immediately to the north of the Temple of Apollo are the conglomerate and limestone remains of a smaller temple, dated to the middle of the 4th century B.C. (see Fig. 40). It has such intimate relations with the slightly later Temple of Apollo Patroos to the south that the divinities worshipped here should be Zeus Phratrios and Athena Phratria. As the principal deities of the ancestral religious brotherhoods, or *phratries*, membership in which was almost a prerequisite of Athenian citizenship, these divinities were closely associated with Apollo Patroos. The altar inscribed to Zeus Phratrios and Athena Phratria, now set up on the base in front, was found on the east side of the excavations. Nothing remains of the superstructure of the little temple, which in its original form was only a cella. The massive foundation to the east, largely made of conglomerate blocks, was for a porch added about the middle of the 2nd century B.C., during the Hellenistic building activity in the Agora.

H. A. Thompson, *Hesperia* 6 (1937), pp. 84–90, 104–107; *Agora* III (1957; reprinted 1973), p. 52; *Agora* XIV (1972), pp. 139–140; C. Hedrick, *AJA* 92 (1988), pp. 185–210.

㉕ STOA OF ZEUS ELEUTHERIOS

To the north of the Temple of Apollo are the remains of the Stoa of Zeus Eleutherios, a colonnade with two projecting wings; the northern end has been largely cut away by the Athens–Piraeus Railway. The distinctive plan of the building was adapted for use in several other Greek cities (Thasos, Megalopolis, Kalauria, and Delos) (Fig. 42). The building dates from the last third of the 5th century B.C. Zeus was honored here as the god of freedom and deliverance. The stoa was also a popular promenade and place of rendezvous; Sokrates is reported by both Xenophon and Plato to have met his friends in

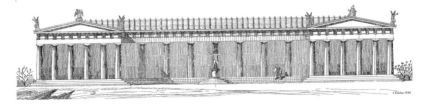

Figure 42. Reconstruction of the Doric Stoa of Zeus Eleutherios, ca. 430–420 B.C.

this stoa for conversation or just to sit or stroll. Of the stoa itself, the poros foundations remain over much of the west side and south end. At the south end also are some step blocks of Hymettian marble. The line of the east front has been fixed from a few surviving blocks and the foundation trench; it has been filled out with modern masonry. Inside the foundations for the west and south walls is a lighter bedding for a continuous bench or couch. Down the middle of the building are square poros foundations for interior columns. The outer, Doric order is represented on the ground by several fragmentary column drums and cornice blocks of white marble; of the inner, Ionic order only very small fragments were found. On the front foundations of the stoa there is also a battered fragment from the poros frieze course, the back of which is lightly stippled; this is a surface treatment that extended over the whole interior face of the wall. A retaining wall of squared blocks was built behind the building to support the steep hillside.

In front of the south wing of the stoa the excavators came upon one almost complete and one more fragmentary marble figure of Victory (Nike) **Ⓜ**. These may have been akroteria from the outer angles of the wing facades. The use of figural akroteria on a stoa is exceptional and is perhaps to be explained by the fact that the Stoa of Zeus was a sacred as well as a civic building. Pausanias (1.3.3–4) records wall paintings by Euphranor—the Twelve Gods, a group of Theseus, Democracy, and the People, and the Battle of Mantinea (362 B.C.)—but of these nothing remains.

Most of the dedications associated with the stoa had some significance for the delivery of the city or the preservation of its freedom. Chief among them was a statue of Zeus Eleutherios (i.e., Zeus of Freedom), mentioned by Pausanias as being in front of the stoa; it stood presumably on the round pedestal of which traces were found on the axis of the building. Shields of warriors who had died fighting bravely in defense of Athens were hung in the stoa; according to Pausanias (10.21.5–6), a number of these were carried off by the soldiers of Sulla after the siege of Athens in 86 B.C.

In Early Roman times the hillside was cut back behind the stoa to make way for a two-roomed annex. Each of the two chambers had its own vestibule approached through the back wall of the stoa; the rooms were paved with marble, and in the southern one was a long statue base. The temple-like aspect of the arrangement was completed by the construction of a large altar in front of the stoa, now exactly overlaid by a marble pile. We may perhaps recognize in the annex the seat of an imperial cult in which successive emperors were worshipped in close association with Zeus Eleutherios; both Augustus and Hadrian in fact bore the epithet "Eleutherios."

Beneath the stoa were found remains (no longer visible) of a small Archaic structure (6th century B.C.) surrounding a rectangular base appropriate for a statue. To the east are slight traces of what appears to have been an altar. This earlier establishment was destroyed by the Persians in 480/79 B.C. From that time until construction of the stoa began, the area was occupied by various industrial establishments such as ironworks and potteries.

📖

H. A. Thompson, *Hesperia* 6 (1937), pp. 5–77; *Agora* III (1957; reprinted 1973), nos. 24–46; J. Travlos, *Pictorial Dictionary of Ancient Athens* (London, 1971), pp. 527–533; *Agora* XIV (1972), pp. 96–103.

26 ROYAL STOA (STOA BASILEIOS)

The northernmost building on the west side of the Agora has come to light in excavations beyond the railway. Since that area is not yet open to the public, we may view it by climbing the stairs behind the Stoa of Zeus and looking down from the railway bridge or from the belvedere to the north of the bridge.

"First on the right," remarked Pausanias (1.3.1) as he entered the Agora, "is the so-called Royal Stoa [Stoa Basileios] in which the royal archon [archon basileus] sits during his year of office." After long years of uncertainty, the point where Pausanias entered the square was established by the excavations of 1970, and the Royal Stoa appeared in precisely the place indicated in his account. It stood near the west end of the narrow area excavated between the railway and modern Hadrian Street to the north.

The royal archon was one of the three principal magistrates of Athens. As the heir to the actual king of earlier days, he had inherited many administrative responsibilities pertaining both to religion and to legal matters: superintendence of the Mysteries, of the festival of Dionysos called the *Epilenaia,* of the torch races, of many ancestral sacrifices, and of lawsuits involving homicide and impiety. It was

Figure 43. Remains of the Royal Stoa, seen from the south

for this reason that Sokrates was required to appear before the royal archon in the stoa when accused of impiety by Meletos in 399 B.C.

From numerous references in the ancient authors we learn much else about the uses of the stoa. On the walls of the building and on stelai in front of it were written the ancestral laws of Athens associated with the names of Drako and Solon and revised at the end of the 5th century B.C. On a stone in front of the building the archons stood each year to take their oath of office, swearing above all to preserve the laws.

In the light of its importance and fame, the Royal Stoa proves to be surprisingly small in scale and modest in design. The plan is a rectangle measuring overall about 7.20 × 17.70 m. Solid walls closed the west, north, and south sides (Figs. 43, 44). Along its front stood eight Doric columns; its interior had four columns of the same order, all of poros. The north wall is preserved to a height of three courses of fine ashlar masonry of poros; the south wall, which had been largely destroyed by the railway in 1891, has been partially restored by the

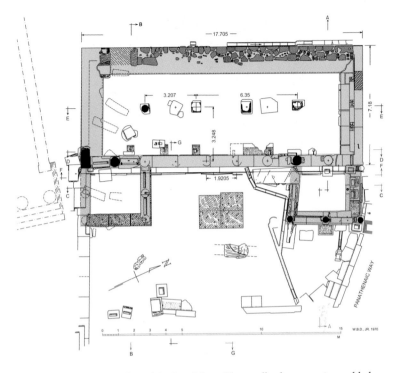

Figure 44. Actual state plan of the Royal Stoa. The small columnar wings added later are highlighted in light red.

excavators. At the foot of the wall on all three sides, but best preserved at the north, is the stone underpinning for a continuous platform about 0.85 m wide and 0.56 m high. Three rough poros blocks at the north end formed part of the core of this platform. Behind the colonnade are various bedding blocks; a series of three blocks regularly spaced behind the midpoints of the three southernmost intercolumnar spaces held wooden posts perhaps for the support of a light barrier to provide some degree of privacy for meetings. The Council of the Areopagus when meeting in the Royal Stoa is reported to have protected itself from intrusion by means of a rope barrier. Of the superstructure little has been found: a couple of Doric capitals, fragments of frieze, cornice, and roof tiles, and, most interesting, some small pieces of the terracotta sculptural groups which Pausanias saw on the roof of the stoa: Theseus throwing Skiron into the sea and Hemera carrying off Kephalos (Figs. 45, 46).

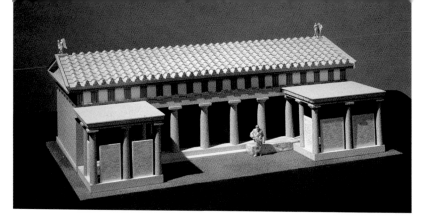

Figure 45. Model of the Royal Stoa after the small columnar wings were added

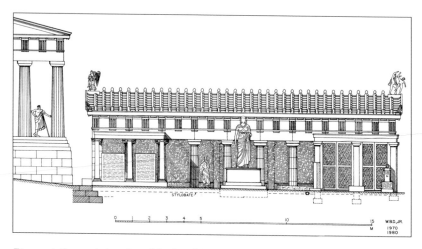

Figure 46. Restored elevation of the Royal Stoa, seen from the east, ca. 300 B.C.

Figure 47. Front
steps of the Royal
Stoa, showing
reused column
shafts in the foun-
dations (now rebur-
ied), view from the
northeast

The area in front of the building was bordered to north and south by banks of stone steps that extended out from the two ends of the facade. At the south three steps remain, at the north, two; their outer ends have not yet been found. These steps permitted the area in front of the stoa to be kept level despite the sloping terrain. Thrones for distinguished guests also existed. A pair of such thrones, made of poros, may be seen where they were reused in front of the north end of the stoa; fragments of a later series, of marble, were also found.

The style of the architecture points to an original date for the stoa in the neighborhood of 500 B.C. The reuse of much old material in the foundations, however, would be more explicable if the building had been erected after the Persian sack of 480/79 B.C. (Fig. 47). There is no clear trace of an earlier building on the site of the stoa. A family burial plot of the Submycenaean period (11th century B.C.) has come to light beneath the south end of the building.

Small columnar wings were later erected against the facade of the stoa, each with three columns on its front. Between the columns of the south wing are sockets for the reception of large marble inscribed slabs (stelai), which in this position would have been easily read from either side. Here were displayed some of the blocks bearing sections of the ancient laws as revised at the end of the 5th century. Several fragments have been found in the Agora excavations, and a nearly complete stele discovered in 1843, inscribed with two sections of Drako's Law on Homicide, was to be set up, according to its own text, "in front of the Royal Stoa." Traces on the surviving masonry at the northwest corner of the building suggest that there may have been a marble facing on the back wall designed to receive the main part of the law code.

The stone *(lithos)* on which magistrates stood to take their oath of office has come to light immediately in front of the stoa, close by the north wing (Fig. 48). It is a massive block of limestone measuring 0.95 m wide, 2.95 m long, and 0.40 m high, roughly trimmed on the sides and worn smooth on top by centuries of use.

On the axis of the stoa and between its two wings is the conglomerate foundation for the pedestal of a large statue. The marble torso was found nearby and is now exhibited in the Stoa of Attalos Ⓜ. Dating from the second half of the 4th century B.C., the figure presumably represents either the goddess Themis, the personification of law and the protectress of oaths, or *Demokratia,* the personification of

Figure 48. The Lithos, or oath-stone, in front of the Royal Stoa, seen from the southeast. The terracotta drain in the foreground dates to the 4th century B.C.; the north wall of the stoa may be seen in the background.

democracy. It was by her side, and with the law codes clearly visible to left and right, that the archons swore to preserve the laws of the city.

In front of the stoa at its north end are several rectangular sockets, some of them cut in marble blocks, others sunk into the reused thrones. In these sockets stood schematic representations of the god Hermes, commonly referred to as Herms. A concentration of such Herms is reported by the lexicographer Harpokration in relation to the Painted Stoa and the Royal Stoa, some erected by private individuals, others by magistrates. The excavations around the Royal Stoa have in fact yielded parts of many Herms ranging in date from the early 5th century B.C. into the 2nd century A.D. The inscriptions, when preserved, record dedications by citizens who had served as royal archons, additional evidence for the identification of the Royal Stoa.

The inscription on the face of the marble Herm base that stands in situ in front of the northernmost column position of the stoa records the names of the poets and producers of the comedy and tragedy that had won the prizes in the year of the dedicator's term as royal archon, a year near the beginning of the 4th century B.C. (Fig. 49). Since at least

Figure 49. Herm base inscribed with the name of the king archon Onesippos, recording winning playwrights and producers in the theatrical contests ca. 405–380 B.C. Found in place on the steps of the Royal Stoa.

one of the producers was not a citizen but a resident alien, these plays were undoubtedly performed at the festival called the *Epilenaia*.

From a well to the south of the Royal Stoa and from a pit to the west of the building have been recovered great quantities of pottery of the 2nd and 3rd quarters of the 5th century B.C. Both cooking vessels and table ware are represented. Many of the bases bear the ligature DE, for *demosion* (state property). From this we may infer the existence somewhere nearby of an official mess *(syssition)* such as is known to have existed in the Tholos and the Prytaneion.

The little building was remarkable not only for the variety of purposes it served but also for its long life. Damaged severely by fire early in its existence, the stoa was rebuilt and enlarged by the addition of the wings, and these in turn underwent many alterations. The debris found above the floor indicates a date of about A.D. 400 for the final destruction and abandonment of the stoa.

Agora III (1957; reprinted 1973), nos. 4–23; T. L. Shear Jr., *Hesperia* 40 (1971), pp. 243–255; *Agora* XIV (1972), pp. 83–90; T. L. Shear Jr., *Hesperia* 44 (1975), pp. 365–374; J. McK. Camp II, *The Athenian Agora* (London, 1986), pp. 53–57, 100–105; *Hesperia* Suppl. 25 (1992).

HERMS IN THE AGORA

Since repeated reference must be made to "the Herms" in discussing the Royal Stoa and the other buildings that stood around the northwest corner of the Agora, we may pause a moment to consider the meaning of the term. In this context "Herm" means a representation of the god Hermes in which the most vital parts (i.e., head and genitals) are rendered naturalistically (Fig. 50) while the trunk and arms are given only a schematic, angular shape. This form of representation was particularly suited to the god Hermes in the discharge of one of his many functions, the guardianship of thoroughfares and entrances. It is not surprising, therefore, that Herms were set up around the northwest corner of the Agora, near the principal entrance to the square. According to a passage in Harpokration, these Herms extended from the Royal Stoa and the Painted Stoa. Many of those beside the Royal Stoa have now been found, and another group has come to light near the Painted Stoa, which stood on the other side of the Panathenaic Way. We hear of a third stoa in this area within which Herms were erected in such numbers that the building came to be called the Stoa of the Herms. A reference by the orator Antiphon shows it to have been standing already by about 425 B.C. A clue to a more precise location of the building was provided by the discovery of two inscriptions of 282/1 B.C. reused in walls of the Early Roman period some 25 to 60 m to the north and northwest of the Royal Stoa; according to their texts, the stelai were to be set up "in the Stoa of the Herms."

The cluster of Herms at the northwest corner of the Agora must have been one of the most distinctive features of the place. "The Herms" are repeatedly given as a point of reference: for the setting up of inscriptions, for the location of a barbershop, for defining the haunts of Sokrates, and for the cavalry officers, as a starting point of equestrian exercises.

The Herms of the Agora were undoubtedly among the prime targets of the Herm-Choppers *(Hermokopidai),* who threw the city into a state of frenzy in 415 B.C. by mutilating the

Figure 50. Three Herm heads found at the northwest corner of the Agora (from left to right): 2nd century A.D., late 5th century B.C., and early 5th century B.C.

Herms on the eve of the departure of the Sicilian Expedition:

> *In the meantime, of the stone Herms in the city of Athens (these square-wrought figures, in accordance with local custom, stand in large numbers both in private entrances and in shrines or in entrance porches, both private and sacred) the majority had their faces mutilated in one single night.* (Thuc. 6.27)

Alkibiades and some of his friends were accused of this and other impious acts. They were executed or went into exile and their property was sold at public auction (see p. 144). Several of the excavated Herms show signs of damage and subsequent repair.

Distinct from "the Herms," but probably not far from them, stood the Hermes of the Agora, a much admired bronze statue of the god. It is said to have been near a gate, which undoubtedly marked an entrance to the Agora, and close also to the Painted Stoa.

Agora III (1957; reprinted 1973), nos. 301–313; *Agora* XI (1965), pp. 108–117; T. L. Shear Jr., *Hesperia* 40 (1971), pp. 255–259; *Agora* XIV (1972), pp. 94–96.

㉗ CROSSROADS ENCLOSURE

Conspicuous in front of the Royal Stoa is the deep channel of the Great Drain, which is here about to issue from the Agora and join the Eridanos River beneath modern Hadrian Street. Also visible are the stone surface gutters of both the western street and the Panathenaic Way, dating to the late 2nd century B.C.

A small shrine in the form of a square enclosure stood opposite the south wing of the Royal Stoa (Fig. 51). The enclosing wall consists

Figure 51. Aerial view of the Crossroads Enclosure (center, left), 5th century B.C.; west road and Great Drain at the top, Panathenaic Way at the right. Lines of the two roads are indicated by the stone gutters, with the Crossroads shrine and well within the angle.

Figure 52. Restored perspective of northwest corner of the Agora showing Cross-roads Enclosure (foreground), Royal Stoa (left), Panathenaic Way (center), Altar of Aphrodite (top, center), and Stoa Poikile (top, right).

of upright slabs of poros once capped by a crowning member. An original doorway in the north wall was subsequently closed because of the rising ground level (Fig. 52). The enclosure dates from the latter part of the 5th century B.C. It was clearly erected around a bold out-cropping of the native rock, which is still visible within the enclosure and which had presumably been a sacred place from earlier times. A mass of votive offerings found within the enclosure (small vases, lamps, loomweights, knuckle bones, jewelry) suggests the worship of youthful female divinities (Fig. 53).

Figure 53. Crossroads Enclosure, with votive offerings as found

The rising ground level gradually obscured the shrine so that by the 2nd century A.D., when Pausanias passed this way, only the much-worn top of the parapet projected, and this failed to attract his attention.

Just to the north of the enclosure opens the mouth of a well with a massive poros curb. It came into use at about the time that the enclosure was built (i.e., the late 5th century B.C.). The well may indeed belong to the shrine since it was used through the 4th and 3rd centuries B.C. as a dumping place for many more votive offerings. Its clearance also yielded part of the archives of the Athenian cavalry corps of the 4th and 3rd centuries B.C., including many lead tablets, each inscribed with the official description and evaluation of a cavalry mount **M**.

Enclosure: T. L. Shear Jr., *Hesperia* 42 (1973), pp. 126–134, 360–369. Cavalry archives: J. H. Kroll, *Hesperia* 46 (1977), pp. 83–140, 141–146; J. H. Kroll and F. W. Mitchell, *Hesperia* 49 (1980), pp. 86–96.

㉘ LATE ROMAN ROUND BUILDING

Above the enclosure were found the remains of a round building of the 5th century A.D.; its southern half had been exposed already by the railway builders in 1891. Its diameter (18 m) was close to that of the Classical-period Tholos, and the presence of buttresses suggests that this building also, like the Tholos in its later life, was domed. Little survived but the rough lower foundations of concrete and a capacious drain which led out from near the center of the floor; this was all removed in 1974. The building had a short existence in antiquity; its ruins supported a wall of the later 5th or 6th century, perhaps for an aqueduct to supply a water mill (see below, pp. 137–138). The purpose of the round building is still obscure.

T. L. Shear Jr., *Hesperia* 42 (1973), pp. 125–126; *Agora* XXIV (1988), p. 60.

㉙ **APPROACH TO THE AGORA FROM THE DIPYLON GATE**

From a vantage point on the railway bridge above the Stoa of Zeus and the Royal Stoa we may contemplate the approach to the Agora that was followed by most visitors and notably by our indispensable guide, Pausanias, in the middle of the 2nd century A.D.

Having come up from Piraeus, Pausanias entered the city of Athens through the principal gate, the Dipylon. Immediately within the gate he noted the Pompeion, the building for the marshaling of the Panathenaic procession, the ruins of which have been fully explored by Greek and German archaeologists. Then followed a sanctuary of Demeter, which may be the source of a statue base signed by Praxiteles and found in 1936 at the north foot of Kolonos Agoraios ㉙.

Pausanias makes particular mention of the stoas that bordered the road from the Dipylon Gate to the Agora (Paus. 1.2.4–5). In front of them, he tells us, stood bronze statues of famous men and women. Behind them he found various shrines, a gymnasium of Hermes, and a sanctuary of Dionysos installed in the house of Poulytion. This house was notorious as the place in which Alkibiades and his companions on a summer night in 415 B.C. had parodied the Mysteries of Demeter and had then gone forth to mutilate the Herms.

The line of the main street followed by Pausanias, together with something of the colonnades that bordered it, has now been explored in its upper course where it approached the Agora. It was clearly an interesting and impressive example of the type of colonnaded street so much in vogue in Greek cities in the Roman imperial period. The roadway proper, with a graveled surface, was 20 m in width, while the stoas were each about 6.50 m wide.

Of particular interest is the southernmost of the colonnades, a two-aisled stoa. With the aid of a plan (Fig. 54), the ruins of its eastern end can be distinguished below us. A solid median wall divided the building into two aisles, of which the northern faced onto the main street and the southern onto a lesser, parallel street that passed close by the north foot of Kolonos Agoraios and gave access to the Sanctuary of Demos and the Graces. The southern colonnade was all of poros with simple Doric columns standing on a single step. The northern colonnade was apparently intended to be similar, but in its final form its columns stood on three steps, the lowest of poros, the upper two of marble. None of the columns of the northern colonnade

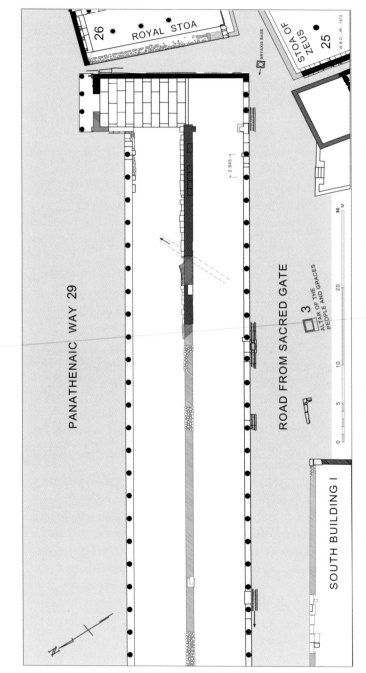

Figure 54. *Stoa northwest of the Agora, facing the Panathenaic Way and the Sacred Way*

has yet been found. Communication between the main street and the lesser street to the south, as also with the lower south aisle of the stoa, was provided by a roofed passageway incorporated into the plan of the east end of the building.

The construction of the stoa probably began in the early 2nd century B.C., but it seems to have continued over a long period with many changes, among which may be noted the partial walling up of the colonnade of the south aisle and the conversion of part of the building into closed shops. Destroyed in the Herulian sack of A.D. 267, the stoa was subsequently rebuilt, only to suffer again in the troubles at the end of the 4th century. Restored again, it continued in use into the 580s.

📖

Street stoas: T. L. Shear Jr., *Hesperia* 42 (1973), pp. 370–382.

③⓪ LATE ROMAN BUILDING

Descending again into the main excavation, we make our way eastward toward the Altar of the Twelve Gods ③①. In doing so we pass through the conspicuous concrete foundations of a large rectangular structure dating from the beginning of the 5th century A.D. A series of rooms on the north, south, and west faced onto a central court, with an entrance at the east. The building is closely contemporary with the Late Roman complex to the south ④①, and the two may have been connected, but no clue has yet been found to the specific function of the northern building.

Beneath the Late Roman building were found remains of at least a dozen monument bases of various sizes and dates. Some of these may well have carried statues mentioned by Pausanias (1.8.3–5) when describing this area.

📖

Agora XXIV (1988), p. 109.

③① ALTAR OF THE TWELVE GODS

Thucydides (6.54) tells us that Peisistratos, the son of Hippias and grandson of the more famous Peisistratos, during his archonship (522/1 B.C.) set up in the Agora an altar to the Twelve Gods. The sanctuary, which consisted of a fenced area, or *peribolos*, with an altar at the center, has been identified by an inscription on a marble statue

Figure 55. Corner of the peribolos *of the Altar of the Twelve Gods, 6th–4th centuries B.C., with the Leagros base at left; view from the south. Most of the rest of the monument lies hidden under the Athens–Piraeus Railway.*

base found in situ against the southwest wall of the enclosure. The inscription reads: "Leagros, son of Glaukon, dedicated [the statue] to the Twelve Gods."

Only the southwestern part of the *peribolos* is visible, the rest being under the railway to the north (Fig. 55). Digging conducted within the railway right-of-way has established the plan. Its location in the open part of the Agora close by the Panathenaic Way made the altar the heart of Athens, the central milestone from which distances to outside places were measured, according to both Herodotos (2.7) and an inscription of the 5th century B.C.: "The city set me up, a truthful monument to show all mortals the measure of their journeying; the distance to the Altar of the Twelve Gods from the harbor is 45 stades [9 km]" (*IG* II^2 2640).

The sanctuary was destroyed by the Persians in 480/79 B.C. and rebuilt toward the end of the 5th century B.C., with additional repairs made in the 4th century. As preserved, the enclosure has a low sill with cuttings and dowel holes for the attachment of a stone fence. This fence surrounded the altar, now missing in the railway cut (Fig. 56).

To the south of the Sanctuary of the Twelve Gods are the remains of a ground altar *(eschara)* of the late 6th century B.C. This type of altar is usually associated with a hero, though this one remains unidentified.

Altar of the Twelve Gods: H. A. Thompson, *Hesperia* 21 (1952), pp. 47–82; *Agora* III (1957; reprinted 1973), nos. 361–378; *Agora* XIV (1972), pp. 129–136; D. Francis and M. Vickers, *PCPS* 207 (1981), pp. 96–136; L. Gadbery, *Hesperia* 61 (1992), pp. 447–489.

Figure 56. Restored view of the Altar of the Twelve Gods

③② ③③ ③④ NORTHEAST SIDE OF THE AGORA

Having completed our survey of the northwest area of the ancient square, we turn now to the northeastern part. Since 1969 the excavations to the north of the railway have been directed toward determining the general line of the north edge of the Agora and distinguishing the various buildings that closed this side of the square in its successive periods. These excavations to the north of the railway are not yet open to the public. From just outside the north gate one gains a general view of the area.

One of the most important results of the exploration in this area is the clarification of the road system in this part of Athens. It is now apparent that the wide road coming up from the main gate of the city, the Dipylon, forked into three branches at the northwest corner of the Agora. The middle branch continued on a southeasterly course diagonally across the square toward the Acropolis; since this was the route followed by the procession in the national festival of the Panathenaia, it was sometimes called the Panathenaic Way. A second branch led almost due south to serve the public buildings on the west side of the Agora. A third branch diverged toward the east. The eastern half of the north side has been sufficiently cleared to permit a sketch of its

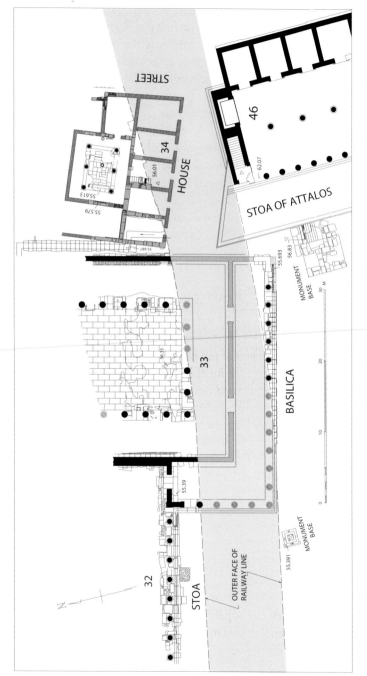

Figure 57. Stoa (1st century B.C./A.D.), Basilica (2nd century A.D.), and Roman house along east half of north side

history (Fig. 57). The earliest phases are represented by a Mycenaean chamber tomb, short lengths of retaining wall that may be as early as the 8th century B.C., and pockets of debris from the Persian destruction of 480/79 B.C. Only in the post-Persian rebuilding does the edge of the square become clearly defined with the erection of a pair of modest buildings comprising rows of one- or two-roomed shops facing south across the square. These appear to have suffered in the Roman siege of 86 B.C. In the 1st century A.D. a large public building was built, of which there has been exposed only a deep Ionic colonnade facing south **32**. Its massive foundations of miscellaneous reused material, salvaged no doubt from buildings destroyed in 86 B.C., overlie the slight remains of the old shop buildings.

Farther to the east one can make out areas of marble flooring. These belong to a large Basilica **33**, erected in the middle of the 2nd century A.D., with its major axis north–south. The Ionic porch of the older building to the west was now extended around the south end of the Basilica in an L-shaped scheme. The consequence of this bold intrusion for the realignment of thoroughfares in this part of Athens and the spatial relationship between the new Basilica and the Library of Hadrian to the east can be clarified only by future exploration.

As yet only the south end of the Basilica has been exposed, but the plan appears to be normal for this type of building. Within a closed rectangle a marble-floored central nave some 15 m wide was surrounded by a corridor 6 m wide. In addition to the marble flooring, many fragments of marble wall revetment and sculpted piers came to light in the excavation. The Basilica is an impressive example of the more closed type of building that came, in the Roman imperial period, to supplement the old open stoa as a place for public intercourse.

To the east of the Basilica are the remains of a substantial house of the Roman period **34**, two stories in height and with a colonnaded court. The plan appears to have included a row of five one-room shops facing south onto the cul-de-sac that remained to the north of the Stoa of Attalos.

Following the Herulian sack of A.D. 267, the area was refurbished in the early 5th century A.D. A pair of parallel foundations bordered the south side of the ancient road in the eastern part of the area. Some of their rough masonry has been left above the floor of the Basilica.

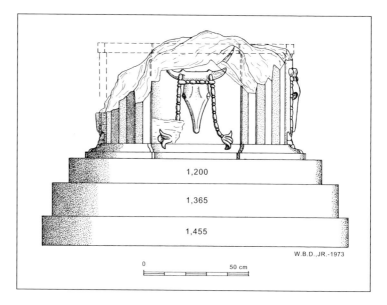

1,200

1,365

1,455

W.B.D.,JR.-1973

0   50 cm

Figure 58. Hellenistic altar with boukranion

These lend themselves to restoration as a colonnade; a corresponding stoa is probably to be restored on the north side of the road.

Prominent in the excavated area to the west of the north gate is a large round altar made of white marble above a two-stepped base of blue marble (Fig. 58). The drum is encircled by a Doric frieze, the four metopes of which were each filled with an ox skull (*boukranion*). The style suggests an Early Hellenistic date, but the altar must have been moved from elsewhere in late antiquity since in its present location it has no proper foundation; it also intrudes on the Panathenaic Way.

T. L. Shear Jr., *Hesperia* 42 (1973), pp. 134–144.

📖 The most recent excavations (begun in 1980) lie beyond the present fenced area of the archaeological zone, along the north side of Hadrian Street. They can be reached by leaving the site through the north gate (the railway bridge) and turning left (west). They appear on the right some 50–75 m down the road.

㉟ PAINTED STOA (STOA POIKILE)

The recent excavations at the northwest corner of the Agora have revealed the foundations of a number of buildings (Fig. 59). The long stepped foundations visible in the middle of the excavated section are the west end of a long stoa; the eastern end of the building is at the northeast corner of the section. Much of the rest is still hidden under modern buildings. Though only partially exposed, enough has

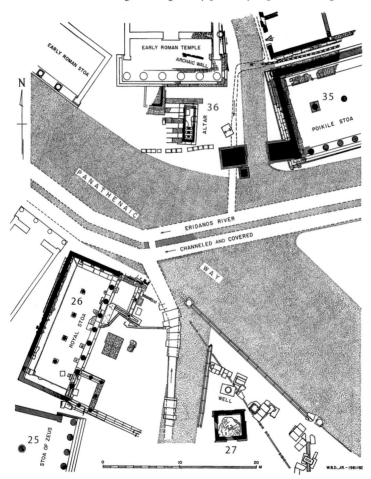

Figure 59. Plan of the northwest corner of the Agora, showing the recent excavations at the top. From left to right: Early Roman stoa; Altar of Aphrodite (6th–5th centuries B.C.); two piers for a gateway (late 4th century B.C.); foundations of the Painted Stoa (ca. 475–460 B.C.).

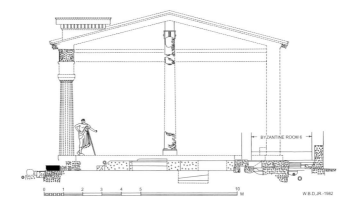

Figure 60. Restored cross section of the Painted Stoa, showing Doric columns outside, Ionic within

been recovered to allow us to restore it as a double colonnade facing south, with Doric columns on the outside and Ionic columns within (Fig. 60). Most of the building was made of different limestones, though the interior Ionic columns had capitals and bases of marble (Fig. 61). The structure is well designed, carefully built, and one of the more lavish secular buildings in Athens. The step blocks, for instance, were all cut to the same length, with the joints fastened by means of iron double-T clamps leaded in (Fig. 62). According to the pottery

Figure 61. An interior Ionic column and base of the Painted Stoa uncovered during the recent excavations

associated with its construction, the building should be dated to the period 475–460 B.C. Of all the stoas of Athens it holds the preferred location, along the north side of the Agora square, looking right up the Panathenaic Way to the Acropolis. It has the southern exposure recommended for stoas in order to take advantage of the warmth of the low winter sun while presenting its back wall to the cold north wind. Pausanias saw the Painted Stoa as he made his way along the north side of the square, and this new stoa corresponds to what we know about the building in terms of size, date, and location; the identification of the remains as those of the Painted Stoa therefore seems probable.

The stoa was first known as the Peisianaktios, after the man responsible for its construction, Peisianax, who may have been the brother-in-law of Kimon. Soon after its construction, however, it was decorated with a series of large paintings, and the building became known by the popular name Poikile (Painted), which appears as its official name in inscriptions by the 4th century B.C.

The paintings were done on large wooden panels *(sanides)* by the outstanding artists of Greece: Polygnotos, Mikon, and Panainos (Fig. 63). The works are referred to time and again by ancient authors and are described in some detail by Pausanias, who saw them still in place after 600 years. They depicted scenes of Athenian military exploits, both mythological and historical: the Athenians against the

Figure 62. Detail of the steps at the west end of the Painted Stoa, ca. 475–460 B.C.

Figure 63. Restored perspective of the west end of the Painted Stoa

Amazons, the Greeks at Troy, the Athenians defeating the Spartans at Argive Oinoe, and—by far the most famous—the Athenian victory over the Persians at Marathon. Pausanias's description is as follows:

> *The last part of the painting consists of those who fought at Marathon. The Boiotians of Plataia and the Attic contingent are coming to grips with the barbarians; at this point the action is evenly balanced between both sides. In the inner part of the fight the barbarians are fleeing and pushing one another into the marsh; at the extreme end of the painting are the Phoenician ships and the Greeks killing the barbarians who are tumbling into them. In this picture are also shown Marathon, the hero after whom the plain is named, Theseus, represented as coming up from the earth, Athena, and Herakles—the Marathonians, according to their own account, were the first to recognize Herakles as a god. Of the combatants, the most conspicuous in the picture is Kallimachos, who was chosen by the Athenians to be polemarch, and of the generals, Miltiades.* (Paus. 1.15.3)

After they were seen by Pausanias in the 2nd century A.D., the paintings were all removed, apparently at the time of the bishop Synesios, who wrote ca. A.D. 400:

May the ship's captain who brought me here perish miserably. Present-day Athens possesses nothing venerable except the illustrious names of places. When the sacrifice of a victim has been completed, the skin is left as a token of the animal that once existed; in the same way now that philosophy has departed hence, all that is left for us is to walk around and wonder at the Academy and the Lyceum, and, by Zeus, the Poikile Stoa after which the philosophy of Chrysippos is named, now no longer many colored; the proconsul took away the sanides *to which Polygnotos of Thasos committed his art.* (Epist. 135)

In addition to these illustrations of Athenian exploits, the stoa housed more tangible reminders of her military triumphs, which were seen by Pausanias:

In the Poikile are deposited bronze shields. On some is an inscription saying that they were taken from the Skionaians and their auxiliaries; others, smeared with pitch to protect them from the ravages of time and rust, are said to be the shields of the Lacedaimonians who were captured at the island of Sphakteria. (Paus. 1.15.4)

The battle of Sphakteria at Pylos in 425/4 B.C. was one of the great Athenian triumphs of the Peloponnesian War; 292 Spartans were captured alive, and their armor apparently remained on public display for close to 600 years. One of the captured shields from the battle has been found in the excavations (Fig. 64). It is round, measuring about 1 m in diameter, with a relief border decorated with a guilloche pattern.

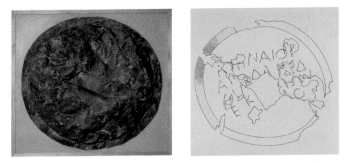

Figure 64. Bronze shield taken by the Athenians from the Spartans at Pylos (425 B.C.) and displayed as a trophy on the Painted Stoa: photograph (left), drawing showing punched inscription and guilloche pattern (right)

The bronze is badly corroded and damaged, so the original weight cannot be determined; presumably there was an inner lining of leather, now missing. The shield was found in a cistern that was filled up in the 3rd century B.C., and it cannot therefore have been seen by Pausanias, although it is certainly one of the same series. This is known because of the punched inscription across the front: "The Athenians from the Lacedaimonians from Pylos."

In addition to displaying paintings and captured arms, the Painted Stoa was used for a wide variety of other functions. Unlike most of the other stoas in the Agora, it was not built for any specific purpose or activity or for the use of a single group of officials. Rather, it seems to have served the needs of the populace at large, providing shelter and a place to meet just off the Agora square. To be sure, it was used on occasion for official functions. A proclamation summoning those qualified to attend the Eleusinian Mysteries was made from the stoa every year, and it was used for legal proceedings as well. Demosthenes mentions an arbitration held here, and inscriptions of the 4th century B.C. refer to full courts of 501 jurors using the building. In addition to its official purposes, the stoa was also used informally by a mixed throng of people. This is clear from the abundant references in the written sources to the frequent use of the stoa by those whose trade depended on a crowd: sword-swallowers, jugglers, beggars, parasites, and fishmongers: "And yet at Athens lately, in front of the Stoa Poikile, with these two eyes I saw a conjurer devour a cavalry sword sharpened to a very keen point" (Apul. *Met.* 1.4). Among those who came regularly were the philosophers, who could expect to find a ready audience in this convenient meeting place. There are references to cynicism and other unspecified philosophies being taught in the stoa, but one branch of Western philosophy is particularly associated with the Painted Stoa. It was founded by the philosopher Zeno, who came to Athens from Kition on Cyprus in the years around 300 B.C. He preferred the Painted Stoa and met here so regularly with his followers that they took their name from this particular stoa, which served as their classroom. Diogenes Laertius, writing in the 3rd century A.D., gives the clearest account: "He used to discourse in the Poikile Stoa, which was also called Peisianaktios, and derived the name Poikile from the painting of Polygnotos. . . . Henceforth people came hither to hear him, and for this reason they were called Stoics."

The stoa, filled with crowds from the Agora and frequented by philosophers, fits well the picture of the kind of liberal and elegant resorts that Kimon is said to have built for the city, a popular *lesche* (clubhouse or hangout) where Athenians came together to discourse, argue, and learn.

Running along the back wall of the stoa was found an aqueduct of large terracotta pipes, carrying water in a westerly direction (Fig. 65). The same line has been found by Greek and German archaeologists farther west, heading toward the Academy, which Kimon is said to have beautified by planting trees and providing water (Plut. *Kimon* 13.8). Given its date, direction, and association with the stoa, this pipeline is probably the aqueduct that watered the Academy.

Figure 65. Terracotta pipeline immediately behind the Painted Stoa, taking water westward toward the Academy, ca. 475–460 B.C.

Behind the stoa are two courses of fine ashlar blocks. These make up the south wall of a row of west-facing square rooms, which opened onto the road that ran northwest along the west end of the Painted Stoa. They are probably small shops dating to the Classical period.

Resting on the steps of the Painted Stoa are the foundations of a pier measuring 2.70 × 3.30 m. Some 2.50 m to the west are similar foundations, not so well preserved and today supporting a much later Ionic column base. Together these two piers originally supported a monumental gate that spanned the narrow street leading off to the northwest. The gate was seen by Pausanias, who describes it just before his account of the Painted Stoa and says that it carried a trophy celebrating an Athenian victory over the Macedonians in 303/2 B.C. Nothing of the superstructure has been recognized and the form of the gate is uncertain.

📖

Stoa Poikile and gate: *Agora* III (1957; reprinted 1973), nos. 47–98; *Agora* XIV (1972), pp. 90–94; T. L. Shear Jr., *Hesperia* 53 (1984), pp. 1–57; J. McK. Camp II, *The Athenian Agora* (London, 1986), pp. 162–165.

㊱ ALTAR AND SANCTUARY OF APHRODITE OURANIA

Just west of the foundations of the gate may be seen the remains of an altar. A platform of hard purplish limestone is preserved, measuring 5.10 × 2.40 m. On top stood the altar itself, although now only its southern half survives (Fig. 66). The core of the altar was made up of soft, yellowish, poros limestone blocks set on edge ca. 0.30 m apart, around which were set orthostates (upright blocks) of white marble from one of the Cycladic islands, probably Paros or Naxos. The orthostates are carved with a handsome molding at their base. The crowning course is missing, though two pedimental end pieces decorated with floral motifs were found nearby and are probably from the altar (Fig. 67). Pottery found up against and inside the base suggests that the altar should be dated to ca. 500 B.C., as does the use of marble from the islands rather than the local quarries on Mount Pentele, which first began to be exploited extensively around 490 B.C.

Its identification as an altar is certain from the form of the monument as well as from the ashes and bones of the sacrifices found inside the core, mostly pigs, sheep, and goats, with an occasional bird. The identification as an altar of Aphrodite seems likely. Pausanias

Figure 66. Altar of Aphrodite, ca. 500 B.C., seen from the south

describes a sanctuary of Aphrodite Ourania (Heavenly Aphrodite) at about this spot after he passes the Hephaisteion and makes his way to the Painted Stoa along the north side of the square: "Nearby is a shrine of Aphrodite Ourania.... The statue still extant in my time is of Parian marble and is the work of Pheidias."

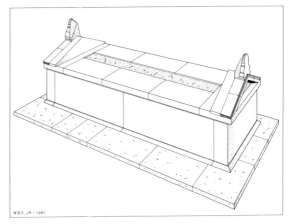

Figure 67. Restored view of the Altar of Aphrodite

Two fragments of a marble relief and assorted figurines of terracotta and ivory found in the area clearly depict Aphrodite and add their weight to the identification. At present the limits of the sanctuary are uncertain. Originally, it may have been a simple open-air shrine with the altar standing alone, though Pausanias's account of a statue carved by the master sculptor Pheidias suggests a temple as well.

Approaching the altar from the east are some foundations of rubble and concrete. They date to the 5th century A.D. and originally supported a colonnade that ran along the north side of the Panathenaic Way in Late Roman times, when the level of the street was much higher.

Behind (north of) the altar are more foundations set at a higher level. They seem to be the foundations for a small prostyle temple of the Roman period that overlooked the area of the altar from the north. (The term "prostyle" refers to it having a columnar porch only across the front.) Excavation along the north side is proceeding to both east and north of the area described here in order to fully expose both the Painted Stoa and the Sanctuary of Aphrodite.

T. L. Shear Jr., *Hesperia* 53 (1984), pp. 1–57; C. M. Edwards, *Hesperia* 53 (1984), pp. 59–72; D. S. Reese, *Hesperia* 58 (1989), pp. 63–70; M. Osanna, *ASAtene* 66–67 (1988–1989), pp. 73–95; Tsakos and Kazamiakis, *Horos* 8–9 (1990–1991), pp. 17–44.

STATUES OF HARMODIOS AND ARISTOGEITON; THE ORCHESTRA

Although a great many monuments that we know about from literary references (and especially from Pausanias) have been identified, there are others for which we have only a general sense of location. The statues of Harmodios and Aristogeiton and the Orchestra are examples. They were probably situated somewhere in the northern area of the Agora, but excavations thus far have failed to identify them.

The assassins of the tyrant Hipparchos in 514 B.C. were Harmodios and Aristogeiton. Although they had been motivated chiefly by a personal grudge, the dramatic circumstances of their deed and of their own subsequent deaths hastened their heroization as the liberators of Athens from despotic rule. Soon after the expulsion of the tyrant's family in 510 B.C., the two men were honored with bronze statues made by Antenor, one of the leading sculptors of the day. These were carried off by the Persians in 480/79 B.C., but they were quickly replaced with a new group made by Kritios and Nesiotes in 477/6 B.C. The first group was sent back from Persia by Alexander the Great or one of his successors, and from then on both groups stood together in a conspicuous part of the Agora. They were the first of many honorary statues to be placed in the Agora.

The only part of the original monument found thus far is a small fragment of the inscribed base for one of the groups **Ⓜ**, which retains part of the epigram: "A great light rose for the Athenians when Aristogeiton and Harmodios killed Hipparchos" (preserved also in Heph. 4.6). Pausanias (1.8.5) recorded the groups not far from the statues that stood around the Temple of Ares. The current excavations may eventually bring to light the base of the monument, though it may have been swept away without having been recorded by the builders of the railway in 1891.

The actions of the tyrannicides were interpreted by the Athenians as a first step in the creation of the democracy. Almost

200 years later, when the democracy was thought to be under threat, the issue of killing a tyrant was raised again. In 336 B.C., soon after the Macedonian king Philip II and his son Alexander (the Great) had crushed Athens at the Battle of Chaironeia in 338 B.C., the Athenians passed a new law which read in part: "If anyone rises up against the People with a view to tyranny or joins in establishing the tyranny, or overthrows the People of the Athenians or the democracy in Athens, whoever kills him who does any of these things shall be blameless." The inscribed stele, decorated with a relief showing Democracy crowning the *Demos* (people of Athens), is on display in the Museum **M**.

According to the lexicographer Timaios, the Tyrannicides stood on the Orchestra. Of the Orchestra another lexicographer, Photios, writes: "The name was first used of the orchestra in the Agora, then of the semicircle at the bottom of the theater, where the choruses sang and danced." From an intriguing reference in Plato's *Apology* (26d–e) we learn that books could be bought at the Orchestra in the time of Sokrates. A clue to the location of the Orchestra within the Agora is given by other testimonia. In the Agora was a famous bronze statue of the Theban poet Pindar. It had been erected by the Athenians in appreciation of a flattering dithyramb he had composed in their honor. This statue was variously located by the ancient authors: in the vicinity of the Temple of Ares (Pausanias) or in front of the Royal Stoa (Pseudo-Aeschines). The site was chosen, perhaps, with reference to the place where Pindar's dithyramb had been performed by a cyclical chorus, and this place was undoubtedly the Orchestra. These indications would appear to locate the Orchestra in the northern part of the Agora.

Tyrannicides: S. Brunnsåker, *The Tyrant-Slayers of Kritios and Nesiotes* (Lund, 1955); *Agora* III (1957; reprinted 1973), nos. 256–280; *Agora* XIV (1972), pp. 155–160. **Orchestra and grandstands *(ikria)***: *Agora* III (1957; reprinted 1973), nos. 524–528; N. G. L. Hammond, *GRBS* 13 (1972), pp. 387–450; *Agora* XIV (1972), pp. 126–129.

㊲ THE PANATHENAIC WAY

Before returning to the main area of the excavations we may pause a moment to look up toward the Acropolis along the line of the broad graveled road, the Panathenaic Way (Fig. 68). Following as it did a natural course for traffic from the principal city gate toward the upper and central parts of the city, the road was in constant use at all times. But it took its name and special character from its role as the route of the procession or great parade of the national festival of Athens, the Panathenaia.

The Parthenon frieze gives a splendid impression of the event, with emphasis on some of its more glamorous aspects: the cavalry, the racing chariots, sacrificial cows and sheep, young men and girls bearing equipment to be used at the sacrifice. On the frieze the spectators of the procession are the heroes of Attica and the gods of Olympus. In actual fact the procession was watched by the citizens of Athens and their guests, for whose convenience on this occasion special wooden grandstands, or *ikria,* were erected in the Agora. Within the Agora proper, the graveled surface on which one walks today is identical with that of antiquity. For the steep stretch between the southeast corner of the square and the upper limits of the Eleusinion ㊶ heavy stone paving was eventually laid, but this was done only in the 2nd century A.D. Drainage channels are visible along the edge of the roadway.

The retention of a graveled surface within the square was probably dictated by other uses of the roadway in connection with the national festival. The normal Greek word for the Panathenaic Way, *dromos,* implies a racecourse, and there is reason to believe that track events originally took place here. A row of square stone bases socketed to hold temporary wooden posts in the line of the Panathenaic Way and to the east of the Altar of the Twelve Gods represents in all probability the starting point for such races (Fig. 69). The installation dates from the second half of the 5th century B.C., at which time, long before the construction of the South Square, a straightaway of the required length (600 Greek feet) would have fit into the open square. A racecourse has also come to light in the middle of the Agora of ancient Argos, and perhaps also at Corinth.

Figure 68. Model of the Agora and northwest Athens in the 2nd century A.D., looking along the entire course of the Panathenaic Way from the Dipylon Gate (bottom) to the Acropolis (top); view from the northwest

Figure 69. Panathenaic Way, just west of the northern entrance to the Agora, showing the starting line blocks (late 5th century B.C.) and cuttings to support wooden bleachers (ikria)

Equestrian exercises also took place on the Panathenaic Way and the cavalry actually trained there:

> *Go forth Manes, to the Agora, to the Herms, the place*
> *frequented by the phylarchs, and to their handsome pupils,*
> *whom Pheidon trains in mounting and dismounting.*
> (Mnesimachos, in Ath. 9.402)

In a remarkable example of a correlation between literary and archaeological evidence, the name of the trainer Pheidon appears on 30 stamped clay discs found in the crossroads well alongside the Panathenaic Way (Fig. 70) **Ⓜ**.

The most spectacular cavalry contest, a sham battle *(anthippasia)* that formed part of the Panathenaic Festival, was held outside the city in the Hippodrome. It is worth noting, however, that parts of several monuments commemorating victories in cavalry displays have come to light in the Agora. One is a base of the 4th century B.C. sculpted by Bryaxis, now in the National Museum; this was found in 1891 in situ just behind the Royal Stoa. Another is a relief with riders found in 1971 near the same place **Ⓜ**. Furthermore, the *apobates* race, in

Figure 70. Clay tokens stamped with the name of Pheidon, the hipparch in Lemnos, who was responsible for training cavalry recruits in the Agora, 4th century B.C.

which a passenger in armor leapt on and off a swiftly moving chariot, continued to take place in the Agora, as we know from inscriptions, at least as late as the 2nd century B.C.; according to Athenian tradition this daring event was the oldest in the roster of the Panathenaic games. The sculpted base of a victory monument for this contest has been found below the Eleusinion (Fig. 71).

Figure 71. Sculpted base for a monument celebrating a victory in the apobates *at the Panathenaic Games, 4th century B.C. As the race made its way along the Panathenaic Way, the armed passenger was expected to jump on and off the moving chariot.*

With the construction of the Panathenaic Stadium outside the city walls in the third quarter of the 4th century B.C., most of the athletic events were undoubtedly transferred from the Agora to that better-appointed setting.

The festival and the procession continued into late antiquity. Himerios, who lived and taught in Athens in the 4th century A.D., gives a vivid vignette of the Panathenaic ship that carried Athena's new robe *(peplos)* to the Acropolis and of "the Dromos, which, descending from above, straight and smooth, divides the stoas extending along it on either side, in which Athenians and the others buy and sell" (Himer. *Or.* 3.12).

Road: *Agora* III (1957; reprinted 1973), nos. 729, 730; *Agora* XIV (1972), pp. 192–203; **Starting line**: T. L. Shear Jr., *Hesperia* 43 (1974), p. 362; **Cavalry and archives**: J. H. Kroll, *Hesperia* 46 (1977), pp. 83–140; J. H. Kroll and F. W. Mitchel, *Hesperia* 49 (1980), pp. 86–96; *AgPicBk* 24 (1998).

Descending again into the main excavation, we turn right.

38 39 THE TEMPLE AND ALTAR OF ARES

The large rectangular area now covered with crushed stone between the Altar of the Twelve Gods 31 and the Odeion 41 represents the solid foundation podium of the Temple of Ares, identified as such by Pausanias (1.8.4). Ares, the god of war, was one of the first divinities worshipped in Athens and was associated with Theseus's defeat of the Amazons. The temple is dated to the third quarter of the 5th century B.C.; a close study of the fragments from the marble superstructure which came to light around the foundations has shown that it was almost a twin of the Temple of Hephaistos on the hill above and was possibly designed by the same architect (Fig. 72). The blocks of the temple foundations are best seen at its east end, while some of the architectural marbles are arranged at the west end of the building (Fig. 73). They include step and wall blocks, column drums, triglyph blocks, and a restored cornice block. These stones bear carefully cut mason's marks, which indicated the exact position of each within the building. East of the temple and on its axis is the foundation of a large marble altar, undoubtedly connected with the temple.

Fragments of a delicately carved marble sima from the Temple of Poseidon at Sounion have been found in the environs of the Ares

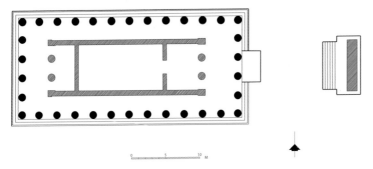

Figure 72. *Restored plan of the Doric Temple of Ares, 5th century B.C., moved into the Agora in Roman times*

temple. The sima (a gutter block from the edge of a roof) was presumably salvaged for reuse on the Ares temple in its new location.

The style of the surviving architectural fragments fixes the date of the original construction of the temple in the 430s B.C.; the altar was added about a century later. The letter forms of the mason's marks, however, are of the Augustan period, as is the latest pottery found beneath the temple foundations. The conclusion is inescapable that the temple, together with its altar, was transplanted toward the end of the 1st century B.C. Where the building originally stood has been

Figure 73. *Architectural remains of the Temple of Ares*

much debated, but seems now to have been Pallene (modern Stavro), where the foundations but no superstructure of a famous temple of Athena have been uncovered. Temple and altar were probably moved on the order of the emperor Augustus, whose adopted son Gaius Caesar is honored in an inscription as "the New Ares."

Temple of Ares: *Agora* III (1957; reprinted 1973), nos. 116, 117; *Agora* XIV (1972), pp. 162–165. **Architecture**: W. B. Dinsmoor, *Hesperia* 9 (1940), pp. 1–52; M. H. McAllister, *Hesperia* 28 (1959), pp. 1–64. **Sculpture**: A. Delivorrias, *Attische Giebelskulpturen und Akrotere* (Tübingen, 1974), pp. 94–161. **Sima from Sounion**: W. B. Dinsmoor Jr., *AJA* 78 (1974), pp. 211–238. **Original location**: M. Korres, *Horos* 10–12 (1992–1998), pp. 83–104.

⓵ SACRED REPOSITORY BY THE PANATHENAIC WAY

Between the Altar of Ares and the Panathenaic Way we look down into a modern stone-lined pit at an underground repository consisting of a stone well curb resting on and surrounded by large reused blocks of poros (Fig. 74). This little cylindrical chamber was originally closed by means of a stopper cut from an old Doric capital and secured by iron clamps (now in the Museum storerooms). When the installation was first made, the top of the stopper was buried to a depth of 0.55 m. Although the pit had been rifled in antiquity, enough of the contents remained to suggest its purpose. The material was evidently of a votive

Figure 74. Sacred Repository by the Panathenaic Way, 5th century B.C.

Figure 75. Small finds from the Sacred Repository

nature, comprising such things as figurines of horses, chariot groups, rectangular plaques for suspension, and shields, all made of terracotta and all appropriate to the worship of heroes (Fig. 75). The offerings had been made in the 7th and 6th centuries B.C.; they were gathered up and buried in the 5th century. It appears probable that the objects had first been dedicated to the heroic dead in one of the many early tombs in the area; the tomb or sanctuary may have been disturbed accidentally in the 5th century, after which the old offerings were piously reburied in the stone container.

H. A. Thompson, *Hesperia* 27 (1958), pp. 148–153; *Agora* XIV (1972), pp. 119–121.

④ ODEION OF AGRIPPA AND LATE ROMAN PALACE(?)

These two large structures, situated south of the Temple of Ares, are closely interrelated. The earlier of the two, the Odeion or Concert Hall, itself preserves the evidence of two periods of construction, but it is in large part overlaid by the later Palace, with which we may begin.

At the north rise four massive pedestals belonging to the Palace. On the north face of the westernmost pier is a set of plans of the building. Made of reused material, the pedestals now support three colossal figures (Fig. 76); of a fourth figure, numerous fragments,

including the head, have been found ⓜ. Originally there were six figures, two on each of the middle piers and one in each lateral position. These statues, conspicuous among the monuments of the Agora, were investigated by the Greek Archaeological Society in the 19th century, when the structure became known as the "Stoa of the Giants." The two fallen westernmost figures were reerected at the same time. Only one of the figures, the easternmost, is actually a giant in the Greek sense of the term, with his legs ending in serpents' tails; the other two are tritons, their human bodies ending in fishes' tails. On the front of the marble base of each figure is carved in relief an olive tree with a serpent twined around the trunk.

The figures in their present position belong to the monu-

Figure 76. Giant from Phase II of the Odeion, mid-2nd century A.D., reused in the facade of the Palace, 5th century A.D.

mental facade of a very large building complex constructed

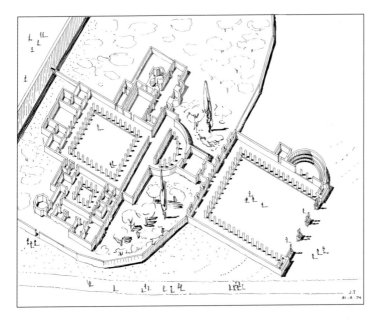

Figure 77. Perspective view of the Palace, early 5th century A.D., seen from the northeast. The giants are at the lower right.

soon after A.D. 400; it covered the ruins of the Odeion and much ground besides, as far south as South Stoa II **65**. The walls, of mortared bricks and rubble stone masonry, are typical of the period. This structure has the characteristic features of a large public residence or palace, with numerous rooms, bathing facilities, courts, and gardens (Fig. 77). It may have served as the seat of a governor or the like. The complex was abandoned in the 6th century A.D.

The Odeion, which had originally occupied the site of the main courtyard of the Palace, was built about 15 B.C. on the axis of the Agora in the area that until then had been part of the open square. It was the gift of M. Vipsanius Agrippa, the minister and son-in-law of the emperor Augustus, and was thus also known as the "theater in the Kerameikos called the Agrippeion." In the original plan the main entrance for spectators was at the south, from the terrace of the Middle Stoa **67**, while the north facade had only a small portico that gave access to the backstage area (Figs. 78, 79).

The orchestra of the Odeion, which is slightly less than a semicircle, is paved with slabs of varicolored marble. At the east, one

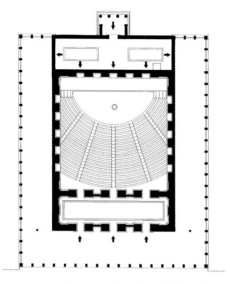

Figure 78. Plan of the Odeion, Phase I, late 1st century B.C.

marble seat of the lowest row is preserved and traces of other rows were found. The auditorium, with a seating capacity of about 1,000, had a span of 25 m and was originally roofed without interior supports; this is one of the boldest ventures in roofing known from the ancient world. The stage, which was decorated with an ornamental front composed of alternating marble slabs and Herms , and the scene building have been walled around with modern masonry to conserve them.

To east, west, and south the auditorium was bordered by a two-storied portico, the lower story being a simple basement, the upper an outward-facing balcony from which citizens might look down on the square. In the southern part may be distinguished the walls and some column stumps of the lower story. Various architectural members belonging to the building have been discovered. A large Corinthian capital from the building was found in 1891 during excavations for the Athens–Piraeus Railway along the north edge of the

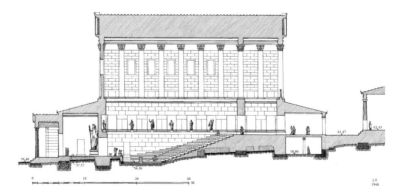

Figure 79. Cross section of the Odeion, Phase I

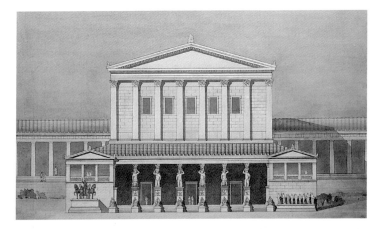

Figure 80. North facade of the Odeion, mid-2nd century A.D., with additions of giants and tritons

Agora; it now stands on the terrace of the Middle Stoa to the south of the Odeion.

The Odeion was seriously damaged around the middle of the 2nd century A.D. when the roof of the auditorium collapsed. It was rebuilt almost immediately, but a cross wall was inserted, which reduced the seating capacity by about half. The north facade was completely remodeled at this time. The small porch was removed and the scene building was turned into a portico. The giants and tritons, originally three of each, were set up as supports for the architrave of the portico, and other sculptural ornament was added (Fig. 80). The torsos of the tritons were copied from the Poseidon of the Parthenon west pediment; the giant follows the type of the Hephaistos of the east pediment. Two draped seated figures, probably portraits of philosophers, which formed part of the sculptural ornament, have been set up to mark the line of the Odeion facade in the mid-2nd century A.D. This rebuilding may be dated to shortly after the visit of Pausanias, who apparently saw the building in its first form, that of a normal odeion. References in Philostratos indicate that in its later form the building was used as a lecture hall.

The Odeion was destroyed by fire in A.D. 267. Most of the blocks were carried off to the east a few years later to be reused in the Post-Herulian Wall, but some bulky pieces not useful as building material were left behind. About A.D. 400, by which time the Athenians had again ventured out beyond the narrow confines of the Post-Herulian fortification, the Palace was constructed in this area. The colossal figures, salvaged from the debris of the Odeion, were moved a short distance to the north of their original positions and were reerected to adorn the new facade.

📖

Palace: H. A. Thompson, *Hesperia* 19 (1950), pp. 134–137; H. A. Thompson, *JRS* 49 (1959), pp. 61–72; *Agora* XXIV (1988), pp. 95–116. **Odeion**: H. A. Thompson, *Hesperia* 19 (1950), pp. 31–141; *Agora* III (1957; reprinted 1973), nos. 520–523; J. Travlos, *Pictorial Dictionary of Ancient Athens* (London, 1971), pp. 365–377.

㊷ MONUMENT BASES EAST OF THE ODEION

The triangular area to the east of the Odeion is thickly strewn with foundations for monuments both large and small. Those toward the south were obviously placed in relation to the terrace wall of the Middle Stoa. A close-set series of small bases must have been aligned with the Panathenaic Way in its final course. The three large bases toward the northern apex of the triangle appear to have taken their alignment from an earlier course of the same road before it was moved eastward by the construction of the Middle Stoa. One of these large bases, the second from the north, is of particular interest since it has the form of a tomb: the joints of the masonry are pointed on the exterior to keep water out, and the roof of the chamber was supported on stone beams. This was conceivably the tomb of some distinguished person who was given the rare honor of burial beneath the Agora.

The inscribed bases for individual statues that have been set up on either side of the Panathenaic Way in this area were recovered by the 19th-century excavators from the Post-Herulian Wall at the south end of the Stoa of Attalos. Dating from the 2nd and 3rd centuries A.D., they record honors paid to individuals by the Athenian state.

The stone water channel bordering the road in this area was laid in the 2nd century B.C.

㊸ MONOPTEROS

West of the Stoa of Attalos in its northern part is a circular building some 8 m in diameter dating from the middle of the 2nd century A.D. (Fig. 81). Three of its decorated cornice blocks survive, along with many fragments from its column shafts of mottled green marble.

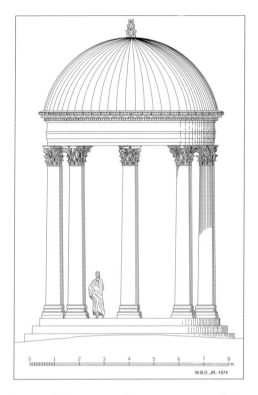

Figure 81. Monopteros, 2nd century A.D., restored view

The ring of eight columns supported a brick dome, one of the earliest known in Greece. There was no wall, hence our building was a "monopteros." This small, colorful building may have sheltered the statue of some divinity.

W. B. Dinsmoor Jr., *Hesperia* 43 (1974), pp. 412–427.

44 EARLY BUILDINGS BENEATH THE STOA OF ATTALOS

Deep beneath the north half of the Stoa of Attalos and extending both to east and west of the stoa are the foundations of a series of public buildings, most of which have been identified as law courts. The identification is based on the discovery among their ruins of various bronze articles known to have been used in the courts, notably a

Figure 82. Inscribed jurors' ballots, 4th century B.C.

small group of ballots, which still lay on the floor in one of the rooms (Fig. 82) , in a container made of two upended drain tiles. This has been interpreted as a "ballot box" into which jurors could deposit their votes (Fig. 83).

The earliest structures of the series, dating from the late 5th and 4th centuries B.C., consisted of unroofed enclosures in which presumably the large juries assembled (Fig. 84). In the late 4th century this old complex made way for a single large building, the Square Peristyle, with colonnades on all four sides of a central court. This building was

Figure 83. "Ballot box" as found, with ballots in situ, under the Stoa of Attalos, ca. 400 B.C.

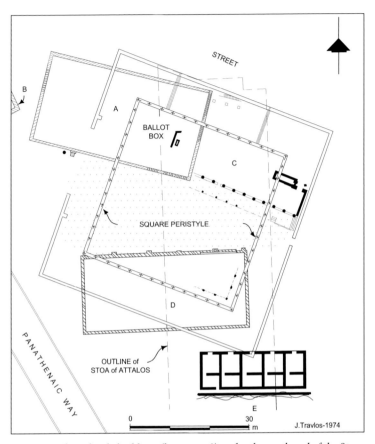

Figure 84. Plan of early buildings (law courts?) under the north end of the Stoa of Attalos

never finished, but it was carried to the point at which much of it could be used, and it did in fact continue in use until demolished to make way for the Stoa of Attalos in the 2nd century B.C. The courts presumably met in the deep porches (Fig. 85).

These buildings have for the most part been reburied for their better protection, but parts have been kept accessible in the basement of the Stoa of Attalos.

A small structure comprising five pairs of rooms on an east–west line stood for a few years between the demolition of the Square Peristyle and the start of work on the Stoa of Attalos; its foundations underlie the central part of the stoa. The plan of the building is

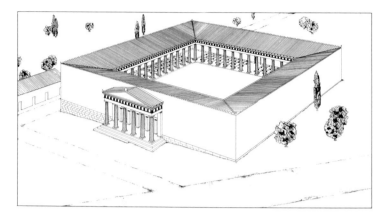

Figure 85. Law court (Square Peristyle) at the northeast corner of the Agora, ca. 300 B.C.

appropriate for shops. Quantities of cooking vessels found in the rear corridor indicated that there were also eating facilities.

Numerous tombs of the Mycenaean and Protogeometric periods came to light in front of and under the Stoa of Attalos; these have been reburied. One of the Protogeometric graves from this area is exhibited in the Museum ⓜ.

📖

Law courts and early remains: *Agora* XXVII (1995); *Agora* XXVIII (1995). **The practice of democracy**: *AgPicBk* 4 (revised 2004).

㊺ BEMA AND DONOR'S MONUMENT

Almost on the axis of the Stoa of Attalos and in front of its terrace wall are two large rectangular foundations. The western has been identified as a *bema,* or speaker's platform ㊺, on the evidence of Athenaeus, who relates that Athenion, "mounting the Bema which had been built for the Roman generals in front of the Stoa of Attalos and standing upon it, looked at the crowd gathered all around." This scene took place in 88 B.C., so construction of the Bema must be dated between that time and the erection of the Stoa of Attalos ca. 150 B.C. Steps led up to the top of the platform at its northwest and southwest corners.

The second monument, set close against the terrace wall of the stoa, presumably honored the donor, Attalos II. More than 100 blocks of its superstructure have been recovered from the Post-Herulian

Wall; they have been stacked along the Panathenaic Way. It was a tall pedestal mostly of Hymettian marble, almost identical with the "Monument of Agrippa" at the entrance to the Acropolis. On top of it stood a life-size four-horse chariot group of bronze at about the level of the second story of the stoa. Many years later, as an inscription from the monument records, the Athenian people rededicated the monument to the emperor Tiberius, just as they rededicated the similar Hellenistic monument in front of the Propylaia to Agrippa.

To both the north and the south of the Donor's Monument is an almost continuous row of bases for other sculpted groups which once enlivened the terrace wall of the stoa.

On our left as we turn in from the Panathenaic Way to enter the stoa stands a massive triangular pillar of Pentelic marble, 2.51 m high. It once supported a bronze tripod. According to the inscription on the side of the base (*IG* II^2 3114), the monument commemorated a victory in choral singing won by the tribe Kekropis late in the 1st century A.D. It was paid for by a joint subscription on the part of both the sponsors (*choregoi*) and the participants. The inscription on the monument reads: "I distribute glory to the contributors in proportion to my debt to each." The base was found in the 20th century standing in the southeast corner of the Stoa of Attalos.

📖

T. L. Shear, *Hesperia* 7 (1938), p. 324; *Agora* III (1957; reprinted 1973), no. 99; *Agora* XIV (1972), pp. 51–52.

46 STOA OF ATTALOS

Let us pause a moment in front of the dedicatory inscription that has been set up at the foot of the stoa terrace wall to the north (left) of the entrance. Carved in large letters, once painted red, the inscription occupied a prominent place on the architrave above the lower story of columns. Although fragmentary, it gives us the name of the donor: "King Attalos, son of King Attalos and of Queen Apollonis," that is, Attalos II, king of Pergamon (159–138 B.C.). Like the princes of several other royal families in the Hellenistic period, Attalos had studied in the schools of Athens as a young man; upon ascending the throne he made this splendid gift to the city of his alma mater (Fig. 86).

The building is an excellent example of the fully developed type of stoa. On each of its two stories a two-aisled colonnade was backed

Figure 86. The reconstructed Stoa of Attalos today, viewed from the north-northwest

by a row of 21 rooms, which served chiefly as shops. In front, a broad terrace ran the whole length of the building (Figs. 87, 88).

The chief function of the stoa was to provide a sheltered promenade for informal intercourse, which must also have assured its success as a shopping center. The shops were no doubt rented by the state to individual merchants, so the building would have served as a source of revenue as well as an ornament to the city. Note the adaptation of the lower, Doric order for a stoa, a building designed for use by numerous people, unlike a temple. These Doric columns are more widely spaced for easy access, and the lower third of each exterior column is left unfluted so as to prevent damage by people and goods passing in and out of the colonnade (Fig. 89).

After undergoing various slight alterations in the course of four centuries, the stoa shared in the destruction of A.D. 267; note the effects of fire on the inner face of the south end wall. A few years later it was incorporated in the Post-Herulian Wall, at which time the facade and all the columns were dismantled to be used in strengthening the rear part of the building (Fig. 90). The back rooms continued in use into Ottoman times. The excavation of the building, having been carried out at intervals during the 19th century by the Greek Archaeological Society, was completed by the American School. In the years 1953 to 1956, the stoa was rebuilt primarily to serve as the Agora Museum (Figs. 91, 92).

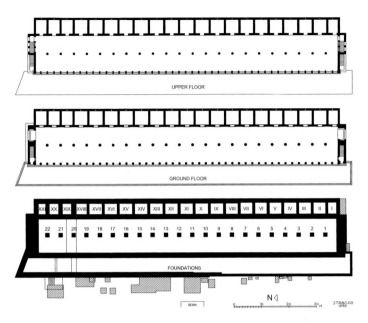

Figure 87. Plan of the interior arrangement of the two-story Stoa of Attalos

Figure 88. Interior view of the lower colonnade of the Stoa of Attalos

Figure 89. Cutaway model of the Stoa of Attalos, showing interior arrangement

Figure 90. South end of Stoa of Attalos, before reconstruction

Figure 91. *The reconstruction of the Stoa of Attalos in 1956, view from the north*

Figure 92. *Stoa of Attalos shown soon after the completion of reconstruction in 1956*

Enough of the walls and architectural members survive to make possible a detailed and certain restoration. Specimens of the various ancient members have been incorporated in the reconstruction, especially toward the south end of the building near the entrance. The restoration has been carried out in the same materials as the original: marble for the facade, columns, and interior trim; limestone for the walls; and terracotta tiles for the roof. The upper floor and the roof are now supported on beams of reinforced concrete enclosed in wooden shells that reproduce exactly the spacing and dimensions of the original beams of solid wood. The design of the wooden doors has been recovered from cuttings in the marble jambs and thresholds, and from the analogy of surviving ancient tomb doors made of marble in imitation of wood.

At the south end of the Stoa Terrace a small fountain has been installed in place of a much larger fountain contemporary with the stoa. The restored fountain and its benches form, as indicated by the inscribed stele set beside them, a memorial to Theodore Leslie Shear, field director of the Agora excavations from their inception in 1931 until his death in 1945.

📖

Agora III (1957; reprinted 1973), nos. 99–102; J. Travlos, *Pictorial Dictionary of Ancient Athens* (London, 1971), pp. 505–519; *Agora* XIV (1972), pp. 103–108; J. McK. Camp II, *The Athenian Agora* (London, 1986), pp. 168–175; *AgPicBk* 2 (revised 1992).

N We leave the stoa through a doorway at its southwest corner and ascend a few modern steps to a small square.

47 STREET TO THE ROMAN MARKET PLACE

When the Library of Pantainos 48 was built (around A.D. 100) the staircase at the south end of the stoa and the exedra (large arched niche) beneath were pulled down to make room for the realignment of the street running eastward from the Panathenaic Way to the Market of Caesar and Augustus, the Roman Agora. This street was not designed for wheeled traffic: it started with a flight of steps that led up to the paved level space between the stoa and the Library of Pantainos. At the eastern end of this paved area stood an archway, of which the threshold block and the lower parts of the piers remain. The archway was embellished with a small fountain, the water for which flowed through a bronze pipe set in the west face of the southern pier (Fig. 93). The little square itself was paved with marble, and at the time of its formation the south end of the Stoa of Attalos was revetted with marble. A large monument stood at the southwest corner of the square facing the Panathenaic Way. The substantial foundations of this base are partly obscured by a tower of the Post-Herulian fortification.

Starting from the arch at the southeast corner of the Stoa of Attalos, a marble-paved street headed directly toward the main entrance to the Market of Caesar

Figure 93. Restored view of the street leading to the Roman market

and Augustus, the so-called Gate of Athena (Fig. 94). A little short of that gateway, however, this east–west street was interrupted by a road descending from the south. Crossing this road, one mounted a monumental stairway to reach the higher ground in front of the Gate of Athena.

The main east–west street, about 10 m in width, was bordered on the south by an Ionic colonnade of the Library of Pantainos, of which the stylobate and some column bases remain in place. A marble gutter in front of the steps carried off rainwater. The colonnade served as a common facade for 12 rooms that varied a good deal in size and shape. Most of the rooms were undoubtedly shops, but several have unusual features that imply other uses. The fifth from the west was particularly outstanding. Its floor and walls were revetted with marble; a long pedestal rose against its back wall; the column bases in the colonnade in front of the room were distinguished by square plinths. Reused at a late period in the front wall of the room is a base with an inscription recording the dedication of a statue of the emperor Trajan (A.D. 98–117) by Herodes, father of the more familiar Herodes Atticus and chief priest of the cult of the emperor. The room perhaps served as a shrine for the imperial cult. Fortune has preserved the epistyle

Figure 94. Stoa along the street leading to the Roman market-place, ca. A.D. 100, looking east toward the Gate of Athena

or architrave (the line of blocks supported by the columns) from the colonnade in front of the fourth room. An inscription on its face tells us that the people built and paid for the *plateia* (the broad street) out of their own revenues. The stoa on the south side of the street (known as the Street Stoa) is to be dated around A.D. 100; its construction is closely interlocked with that of the Library of Pantainos **48**.

Deep beneath the remains of the stoa of Roman date lie the foundations of several earlier buildings dating from the end of the 5th and from the 4th centuries B.C. The plan of one, comprising a double row of rooms such as are commonly found in shop buildings, suggests the commercial use of this part of the city already in the Classical period.

The contents of a well abandoned in the early 4th century B.C. attest the existence of eating and drinking establishments as well as of local industries such as the working of bone and horn and the making of terracotta figurines.

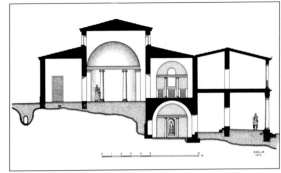

Figure 95. Cross section of the Late Roman Building, incorporating the earlier Street Stoa, 5th century A.D.

The colonnade and related rooms suffered in the sack of A.D. 267, but extensive rebuilding took place in the early 5th century (Figs. 95, 96). From this period dates the suite of three prominent and well-preserved rooms behind the line of the old colonnade (Fig. 97). One entered the series of communicating rooms through a doorway in the north wall of the middle room. The western room, with a marble floor, marble wall trim, and wall niches for statues, was evidently the principal chamber. No clue has been found to the use of the rooms. At a higher level to the south are the remains of a large houselike building, which once extended over the

Figure 96. Elevation of the Street Stoa with the addition of a second story, 5th century A.D.

Figure 97. Suite of basement rooms, early 5th century A.D.

suite of basement rooms. One can distinguish a colonnaded courtyard and a large apsidal room. The old colonnade bordering the street was at least partly restored in this period, with the addition of a second story, as shown by the discovery of many members of a small upper Ionic order with cuttings for a parapet.

The subsequent history of the area is well documented by stratified deposits running down into the 8th century. This contrasts with the history of the region of the old Agora proper, which lay outside the Post-Herulian Wall; there one finds little evidence of habitation after the barbarian inroads of the 580s.

T. L. Shear Jr., *Hesperia* 42 (1973), pp. 144–146, 385–398; T. L. Shear Jr., *Hesperia* 44 (1975), pp. 331–374.

48 LIBRARY OF PANTAINOS

The next building to the south of the Stoa of Attalos was the Library of Pantainos. The Library was almost completely demolished by the builders of the Post-Herulian Wall, which follows the line of the western colonnade of the Library at this point. The most important of the blocks incorporated into the fortification wall is the inscribed lintel of the main doorway of the Library (in the east face of the wall, near the center). The inscription tells us that a certain Titus Flavius Pantainos, his son, and his daughter gave "the outer colonnades, the peristyle, the library with its books, and all the furnishings at their own expense." The inscription may be dated close to the year A.D. 100. A second inscription found in the area contains regulations for the use of the

Figure 98. Library rules, ca. A.D. 100

Library **M**: "No book is to be taken out since we have sworn an oath. (The library) is open from the first until the sixth hour" (Fig. 98).

The main element of the building was a large square room at the east, its floor and walls once revetted with marble (Fig. 99). Its walls are preserved only a little above floor level, but they were probably thick enough to have contained the cupboards in which the book rolls of papyrus and parchment would have been stored. This room faced westward through a row of columns onto a colonnaded courtyard: a pleasant place to stroll, to read, or to reflect. This peristyle was bordered on north and west by rooms which probably had no connection with the Library as such, unless to add to its revenues by rental. The suite of two rooms at the south end of the western range was certainly used as a sculptor's studio. The excavators came upon quantities of marble chips, emery for the polishing of marble, and several pieces of sculpture.

The "outer colonnades" of the dedicatory inscription are readily recognized in the Ionic stoas that faced westward onto the Panathenaic Way and northward toward the Stoa of Attalos and along the east–west street (Fig. 99). These more visible parts of the building were executed

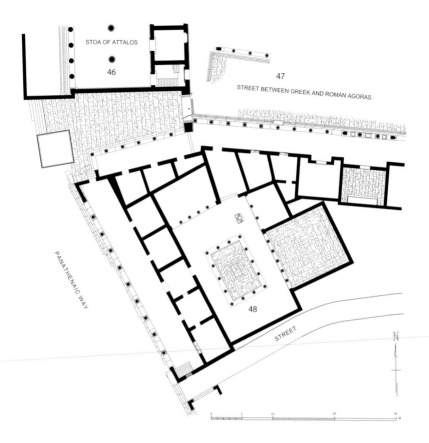

Figure 99. Plan of the Library of Pantainos, A.D. *100*

in worked marble of very respectable quality, in striking contrast to the shabby rubble masonry of the inner walls.

An ancient library was commonly adorned with appropriate sculpture. It is tempting, therefore, to associate with the Library of Pantainos the personifications of the *Iliad* and the *Odyssey* that were found nearby ⓜ, although no appropriate pedestal has yet been found within the building.

Library: J. Travlos, *Pictorial Dictionary of Ancient Athens* (London, 1971), pp. 432–435; *Agora* XIV (1972), pp. 114–116; J. McK. Camp II, *The Athenian Agora* (London, 1986), pp. 187–191. **Dedicatory inscription**: *Hesperia* Suppl. 8 (1949), pp. 268–272; *Agora* III (1957; reprinted 1973), no. 464.

49 POST-HERULIAN WALL

Having traversed the Library of Pantainos from north to south, we turn west across the line of the Post-Herulian Wall. After the Herulian raid in A.D. 267, the Athenians, seeing that the Roman armies were no longer able to protect the frontiers and that they themselves were unable to defend the long circuit of their ancient walls, built a new and much shorter inner circuit. To hasten the work they used blocks from buildings that had been destroyed or badly damaged in the barbarian raid (Fig. 100).

Starting at the so-called Beulé Gate, near the present entrance to the Acropolis, this wall follows the line of the Panathenaic Way down the hill, past the Eleusinion and the Library of Pantainos, to the Stoa of Attalos. In this stretch there were three gates, each set in the line of an earlier street. In the Stoa of Attalos area there were three towers, a huge one at the north, a smaller one near the middle built from blocks of the Donor's Monument and the Bema, and a third at the south. All three have now been demolished. The tower at the south

Figure 100. Late Roman fortification wall (ca. A.D. 280), built of reused material after the destruction of the Agora by the Herulians in A.D. 267. Note Doric column drums at left, in shadow, from the Southwest Temple.

end of the stoa was one of a pair flanking a gateway and was built almost entirely of inscribed monuments from the Agora. It was later converted into a chapel of the Panaghia Pyrgiotissa (Our Lady of the Tower) and was demolished about 1860. The tower at the south side of the gate still stands.

From the north end of the Stoa of Attalos the fortification wall turned east (a section of it is visible behind the stoa) and continued to the Library of Hadrian, which it incorporated as it had the Stoa of Attalos. Beyond the Library of Hadrian it ran east for about 200 m and then turned south. This wall has been known to archaeologists for many years. Opinions as to its date have ranged from the mid-3rd century A.D. (i.e., Valerian) to the 15th century (Frankish). Actually, as the excavations have shown, construction was begun after the disaster of A.D. 267 and was still in progress at least as late as A.D. 280. Various wealthy Athenians of the period were made responsible for the different sections. An inscription found near the east gate (*IG* II² 5199) gives the credit for its building to Claudius Illyrius. Another (*IG* II² 5200), found by the gate at the south end of the Stoa of Attalos, has been translated by Christopher Wordsworth: "Nor Cyclopean hand with labor strong this pile did raise, nor Amphionian song."

The wall shows evidence of repairs (hence the various dates suggested for its construction) and seems to have remained in use until Ottoman times.

The best-preserved stretch of the fortification now visible is that just south of the Stoa of Attalos, where there are two towers and the curtain between them. The wall, with an average thickness of about 3.5 m, had well-built outer and inner faces enclosing a more loosely packed core. It consisted entirely of reused materials: architecture, sculpture, and inscriptions. Note a pair of Ionic columns of white marble extracted from the wall in 1959 and now laid in front of it; a third column of the same series has been set up in the Museum **Ⓜ**. The most characteristic is a series of Doric columns slightly smaller than those of the Temple of Hephaistos. A bottom and top drum and a capital from one of these columns have been assembled at the corner of the Southeast Temple; other drums remain in the wall. The style and quality of workmanship point to a date in the latter part of the 5th century B.C. These columns have been shown to derive from a building at Thorikos on the east coast of Attica; they were presumably removed and brought to Piraeus by sea and reused in the Southwest Temple ⑳ in the 1st century A.D., at a time when Thorikos was already desolate.

Post-Herulian Wall: *Agora* XXIV (1988), pp. 5–11. **Thorikos material**: W. B. Dinsmoor Jr., *Hesperia* 51 (1982), pp. 410–452.

㊿ LATE ROMAN WATER MILL AND OIL MILL

A little to the west of the Post-Herulian Wall are the remains of a water channel built of rubble masonry. One can follow this channel northward for about 30 m to its present end near a slotlike structure about 5 m long and 4 m deep. In the east wall of this pit is an arched aperture that opens into an adjoining room. These are the remains of a water mill. The channel carried the water necessary to turn the wheel, which revolved in the slot or race. The axle of the wheel was housed in the socket and passed through the opening in order to turn the millstones, which then ground the flour in the neighboring room (Fig. 101). The wheel was of the "overshot" variety, as the heavy lime deposit north of the axle line makes clear. The mill mechanism seems very close to that described by Vitruvius (10.4–5), even though the

Figure 101. Perspective drawing of the water mill, 5th–6th century A.D.

Agora mill is some centuries later. Several of the disclike millstones, much worn, were found in the room, together with hundreds of small bronze coins that had fallen through cracks in its wooden floor. The mill was in operation from soon after A.D. 450 to about A.D. 580, and is one of the earliest water mills in Europe of which we have detailed knowledge. This was only one in a chain of three mills turned in succession by the same water. The water came down from the south in an aqueduct. First it turned a mill of which the wheel pit was sunk through the porch of the Southeast Temple (52). Continuing northward the water next operated the well-preserved mill that we have just visited. From here the water was conveyed in a northwesterly direction in a channel at first underground and then supported on arches to supply the third mill, which was totally destroyed by the construction of the railway in 1891.

On the other side of the Panathenaic Way from the water mill are the remains of a contemporary mill for making olive oil. Two elements have survived. A massive drum of volcanic stone formed the lower part of a grinding machine in which the olives were reduced to pulp. Nearby lies a marble block on which the bags of pulp were piled and then subjected to pressure, no doubt by means of a beam anchored at one end; the oil flowed into a channel surrounding the top of the block and thence into a container.

Water mill: A. Parsons, *Hesperia* 5 (1936), pp. 70–90; R. Spain, *Hesperia* 56 (1987), pp. 335–353; *Agora* XXIV (1988), pp. 80–81.

(51) SOUTHEAST STOA

South of the Library of Pantainos, and separated from it by a narrow street, stood another public building that faced onto the Panathenaic Way. At present only the front of the building is accessible, a continuous deep porch of the Ionic order. Excavations made in 1965 in the garden of the large 19th-century house to the east (believed to have belonged to the Colettis family, which gave Greece an early prime minister, 1844–1847) revealed the plan of the rear part: a simple row of 11 one-roomed shops (Fig. 102). The outer face of the Post-Herulian Wall rests directly on the stylobate of the earlier building, but one can easily recognize tumbled parts of all the elements of the facade: the square plinths and round bases on which the columns stood, the

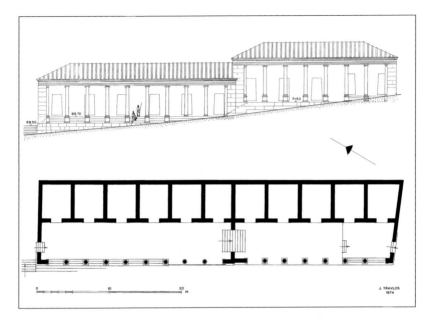

Figure 102. Plan and elevation of the Southeast Stoa, mid-2nd century A.D.

smooth shafts and the capitals of the Ionic columns, the epistyle, and the cornice. Coming from the Panathenaic Way, one normally entered the porch of the building near its midpoint, where the level of the floor coincided with the level of the sloping street. In this prominent part, the stylobate is of marble rather than of poros, which is used in the rest of the stylobate. Because of the sloping terrain, the part of the colonnade to the south of the entrance rested at a level a meter or more above that of the northern part. Stairs in the middle and at both ends of the porch enabled one to traverse its full length and to continue down into the corresponding porch of the Library of Pantainos. The building dates from the middle of the 2nd century A.D.

If the light is right, one may distinguish the graffiti on the shaft of a column of the Southeast Stoa that stands upright in the area of its porch: profiles of human faces, hunting scenes, Herms, and sundials (Fig. 103).

H. A. Thompson, *Hesperia* 29 (1960), pp. 344–347; R. R. Holloway, *Hesperia* 35 (1966), pp. 79–85; *Agora* XIV (1972), p. 109.

Figure 103. Graffiti and doodles on a column of the Southeast Stoa

52 SOUTHEAST TEMPLE

The paving of the Panathenaic Way, dating from the 2nd century A.D., is especially well preserved in front of the Southeast Stoa; note the deep wheel ruts. A number of buildings flank the road at this point (Fig. 104). On the west side of the street opposite the Southeast Stoa are the slight remains of a temple of the Early Roman period. The plan comprised a cella and a north porch of eight columns looking down the Panathenaic Way (Fig. 105). Near the middle of the cella is a mass of rough masonry that formed the core of a large statue base. Scattered bedding blocks attest to a floor of marble slabs in the front part of the cella. The side and back walls of the cella were of rubble

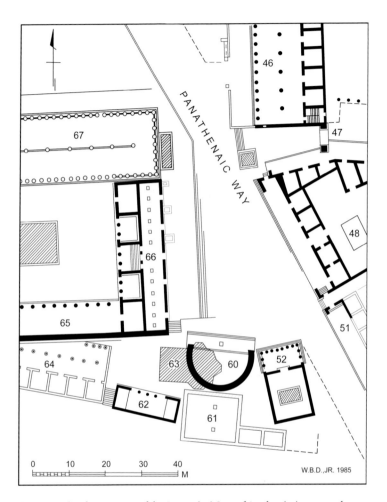

Figure 104. Southeast corner of the Agora: (46) Stoa of Attalos; (47) street to the Roman Market; (48) Library of Pantainos; (51) Southeast Stoa; (52) Southeast Temple; (60) Nymphaion; (61) Mint; (62) Southeast Fountain House; (63) Church of the Holy Apostles; (64) South Stoa I; (65) South Stoa II; (66) East Building; (67) Middle Stoa

masonry once covered with stucco. The foundations for the porch, in contrast, were massively built of reused squared blocks.

Certain elements from the superstructure of the porch have been recognized among the reused material in the adjacent part of the Post-Herulian Wall. These include Ionic columns of a temple of Athena of the 5th century B.C., which originally stood at Cape Sounion.

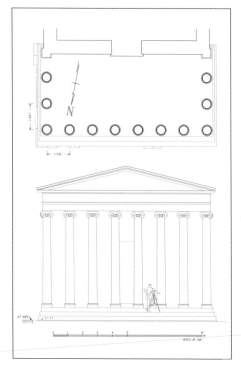

Figure 105. Restoration of Ionic architectural elements from the Temple of Athena at Sounion (5th century B.C.) reused in the Southeast Temple in the Agora, late 1st century A.D.

Within the cella of the temple the excavators came upon three fragments of a colossal marble statue, a heavily draped standing female figure which undoubtedly stood on the great pedestal. The two larger fragments are now sheltered by a roof to the south of the temple. The stance and drapery style are close to those of the Caryatids of the Erechtheion, though the scale is twice as great. The Agora statue may be recognized as an original work of the late 5th century B.C.

Long after the temple was destroyed and its stonework plundered by the builders of the Post-Herulian Wall, the wheel pit of a water mill was set deep down in the area of its porch. This was the uppermost in the chain of three water mills, the best preserved of which we have just encountered.

H. A. Thompson, *Hesperia* 29 (1960), pp. 339–343; W. B. Dinsmoor Jr., *Hesperia* 51 (1982), pp. 410–452.

⑤③ ⑤④ ⑤⑤ AGORA TO ELEUSINION

The Eleusinion and the various monuments on the north slope of the Areopagus are outside the fenced enclosure of the Agora excavations and may be visited free of charge. The visit, however, is recommended only to specialists because the remains are difficult to decipher.

The Panathenaic Way continues upward with a gentle slope to issue from the southeast corner of the Agora. Just beyond this point, the Way is crossed by the road that skirted the south side of the Agora and led into the eastern parts of the city. This roadway was respected by the builders of the Post-Herulian Wall, who left a gateway on its line. At the south side of the gate, and close against the face of the fortification wall, are the remains of a small fenced sanctuary ❸ sacred no doubt to some divinity of the crossroads such as Hekate. South of the crossroad the paved Way continues at a steeper gradient, too steep for most wheeled traffic.

In the southeast angle between the Panathenaic Way and the east–west street are slight remains of what appears to have been another modest sanctuary ❺. The enclosure wall, of conglomerate, dates from the Hellenistic period. One round and several rectangular monument bases have come to light within the enclosure. The whole area has been very much disturbed, and no clue has been found for the identification of the cult. In the Roman period, presumably after the cult had been abandoned, a row of rooms, four large and one small, was inserted into the west side of the area; only the concrete foundations remain. These are most probably shops. To the west the Panathenaic Way is bordered by the remains of an aqueduct ❺. The massive concrete piers must have supported arches of stone masonry on which would have rested the water channel at a level sufficiently high to assure an effective head of water at the ornamental fountain house *(nymphaion)* inside the southeast corner of the Agora ❻. The upward course of the aqueduct may be followed to a square settling basin and thence eastward beneath the Panathenaic Way on a line parallel to the back wall of the stoa that closed the south side of the Eleusinion ❺; in this stretch the water was carried in an underground channel vaulted in brick. The source of the water was presumably the Hadrianic water system completed in A.D. 140. The stonework of the aqueduct bordering the Panathenaic Way was stripped away to be reused in the Post-Herulian Wall in the late 3rd century. In the 5th century this section of the aqueduct was rebuilt in a crude style to supply the needs of the new establishments that had arisen in the Agora; some of the underpinning of this later period may be seen above the concrete piers of the earlier.

📖

Crossroads shrine: H. A. Thompson, *Hesperia* 28 (1959), pp. 91–108.

⑤⑥ ELEUSINION

The sanctuary called the Eleusinion was an Athenian annex of the great shrine of Demeter and Kore at Eleusis to which the initiated made their pilgrimage each year along the Sacred Way. It was among the most venerable sanctuaries of Athens. Each year, on the day following the celebration of the Mysteries, the Council of 500 held a session in the Eleusinion. The spacious sanctuary was protected by a strong wall; for this reason it was one of the few places apart from the Acropolis not to be occupied by refugees in the early years of the Peloponnesian War (Thuc. 2.17.1).

After long speculation the site of the sanctuary has been fixed by excavations along the east side of the Panathenaic Way on the north slope of the Acropolis, about halfway between the Stoa of Attalos and the Propylaia (Fig. 106). Various discoveries combine with the evidence of Pausanias and other literary sources to make the identification certain. Inscribed dedications to the Eleusinian deities have been found on the site, as well as deposits of ritual vases particularly sacred to Demeter and Kore; these had been dedicated to the goddesses and later were carefully buried by the priests when room had to be made in the shrine for more. From this area have come to light many pieces of the stelai recording the sale of property confiscated from Alkibiades and others accused of mutilating the Herms and parodying the Eleusinian Mysteries; the stelai are known to have stood in the Eleusinion. The eastern limit of the sanctuary has not yet been excavated.

Near the middle of the excavated area is a rectangular building with one large room, restored with four columns in front of each end (*amphiprostyle*) (Fig. 107). The entrance to the main room was probably through its south end. Because of the steeply sloping site, the north end of the building was supported on a massive foundation of Kara limestone very carefully worked. During construction the plan was altered and the building was extended eastward. The style of the masonry and the evidence from stratification point to a date early in the 5th century B.C. for the platform, and the temple may have been finished in the second quarter of the century.

The south end of this building disturbed the north wall of an early *peribolos* dating from about the middle of the 6th century B.C. The best-preserved part of this early enclosure is a length of massive wall

Figure 106. View north from high on the slopes of the Areopagus down the Panathenaic Way. On the right of the road are remains of the Eleusinion and on the left remains of several large houses of late antiquity.

of Acropolis limestone along its west side. In the latter part of the 5th century B.C., a long, narrow pedestal was erected to the east of the temple. It conceivably supported the series of 10 or more marble stelai on which was recorded the sale of the property of those who profaned the Mysteries of Demeter in 415 B.C. In the 2nd century B.C., a marble gateway was built at the southwest corner of the sanctuary and a stoa, presumably Doric, was built along the south side.

An east–west roadway bordering the south side of the Eleusinion separated the main sanctuary from a less well-defined area on a ledge in the rising hillside. Toward the southeast corner of this area are

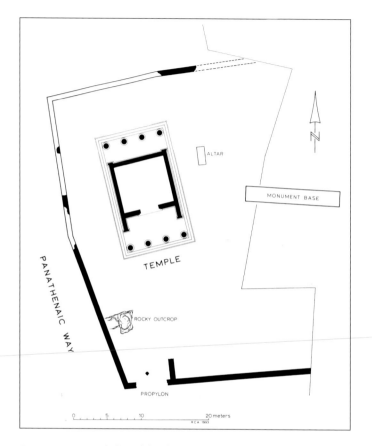

Figure 107. Restored plan of the Eleusinion, mid-5th century B.C.

the ill-preserved remains of a small round structure of Early Roman date made of reused blocks. The discovery of four small poros altars in the vicinity of the round structure suggests that we are dealing with a sanctuary, perhaps one related to the Eleusinion proper (the altars are now on the terrace of the Stoa of Attalos); several of the deposits of ritual vases noted earlier were found within the limits of this area. Pausanias (1.14.1), after describing a fountain house called the Enneakrounos, noted that "there are two temples above the fountain house; one belongs to Demeter and Kore; in the other, that of Triptolemos, there is a statue of him."

After a digression on Triptolemos, Pausanias refers to "the sanctuary at Athens called the Eleusinion" and then again mentions the temple in which was the statue of Triptolemos. He was prevented by a dream, he tells us, from revealing more about the Eleusinion. This dream has not only deprived us of an account of the sanctuary but has also left uncertain the relationship between the two temples and the Eleusinion. It seems likely that the excavated temple is that of Triptolemos, and that the main buildings of the Eleusinion still lie buried farther to the east.

📖

Agora XXXI (1998).

57 58 59 THE NORTH SLOPE OF THE AREOPAGUS

Those who have made their way up as far as the Eleusinion, and who have sturdy shoes, may wish to explore the north slope of the Areopagus (see Fig. 1). The excavation of this vast area has yielded little of interest for the Classical period, but it has added much to some of the earliest and to some of the latest chapters in the history of Athens.

Through the Mycenaean, Protogeometric, and Geometric periods (14th–8th centuries B.C.) the hillside was used as a burial ground. Particularly noteworthy were the large Mycenaean chamber tomb of about 1400 B.C. opened in 1939 on the northeast shoulder of the Areopagus, and the richly furnished grave of a woman of the 9th century B.C. found in 1967 at the north foot of the hill. The crumbly nature of the rock has made it necessary to refill all the tombs, but the principal groups of grave furnishings are exhibited in the Museum Ⓜ.

From the 6th century B.C. onward habitation is attested. Throughout later antiquity, the hillside was a thickly settled residential area served by a main road that ran westward from the Eleusinion following the contours of the hillside. The long continuity of habitation has tended to obliterate the remains of earlier periods, but house plans of the 6th–5th centuries B.C. have been recovered in a block near the middle of the lower slope. The individual houses were modest both in scale and furnishings: two to eight rooms grouped informally around a small courtyard without porches.

More conspicuous and more readily intelligible are the remains of several large houses of late antiquity that can be reached easily by leaving the Panathenaic Way and proceeding westward from the Eleusinion. We pass on the right the exiguous remains of a number of shabby houses, some of which were occupied by marble workers

Figure 108. Restored plan of the Omega House, on the slopes of the Areopagus, 4th century A.D.

in the 2nd and 3rd centuries A.D. Then we look down onto the foundations of a large house **57**, the central element in which was a room with a semicircular apse toward the south. To the east and west were courtyards, that to the east having a complete peristyle with a well in the middle of the court; rooms of various sizes, some 20 in all, were grouped around the courtyards. Farther to the west and lower down is another house of comparable plan. These were perhaps the residences of successful teachers (sophists) of the 4th and 5th centuries A.D., some of whom are reported to have provided lodgings in their own houses for their favorite pupils and to have done their teaching at home in well-appointed lecture rooms. On the other side of the road and above the first house with the apsidal room are the remains of another extensive residence known as the Omega House **58** (Figs. 108–110).

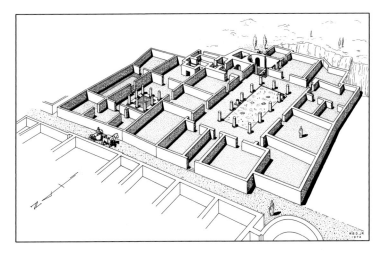

Figure 109. Partially restored perspective of the Omega House from the north-west, 4th–6th centuries A.D.

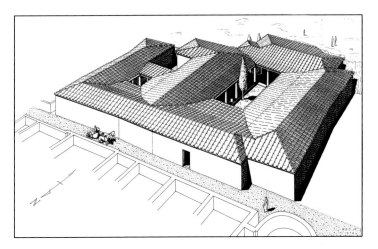

Figure 110. Fully restored perspective of the Omega House

Already in the 4th century B.C. the site had been occupied by a substantial house, but the remains one now sees belong chiefly to the 4th and 5th centuries A.D. This house also boasted two courtyards, and it had besides a bathing area with hot and cold rooms. Most elegant, however, is a curious apartment opening off the south side of the main

Figure 111. Pool and arched niches of the Omega House, from the west

colonnaded courtyard of the house (Fig. 111). Descending by a flight of steps flanked by columns, one entered an apsidal room that once glowed with the rich colors of a mosaic floor and marble-revetted walls. The mosaic, in an elaborate geometric design, is confined to the rectangular part of the room. The apse, toward the east, was covered with a half dome, and in its floor was a semicircular stepped basin. Water was supplied by a natural spring farther to the east, which had been exploited by the property owners in various ways for centuries. The room was probably a triclinium, a cool retreat for summer dining, with couches placed on the mosaic. We should have expected the panel within the mosaic borders to have been occupied by a mythological scene likewise done in mosaic, and this was probably the original arrangement. The panel is now filled with *opus sectile* (small plaques of colored marble) of coarse workmanship in which the central motif is a cross executed in deep red stone (Fig. 112).

It may be that the cross is symbolic and an indication that the owners of the house were now Christian. Conversion, or a change of ownership from pagan to Christian, is attested at the same time by the treatment accorded a rich collection of sculpture that had previously adorned the house. A number of pieces, including a head of Nike, a

Figure 112. Mosaic floor of the Omega House, 4th century A.D., central panel reset in the 6th century A.D.

statue of Herakles, a bust of Helios, a bust of the emperor Antoninus Pius, and three private portrait busts, were deposited in two wells, which were then closed, while on a votive relief which remained above ground the heads of the pagan divinities were deliberately mutilated **Ⓜ**. All this happened in the first half of the 6th century A.D., when pagans were forbidden by the emperor Justinian to teach philosophy at Athens; the house itself was not destroyed until the Slavic invasion of the 580s.

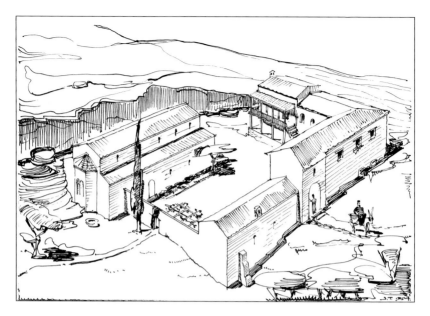

Figure 113. Church of St. Dionysios on the slopes of the Areopagus, 16th century A.D.

Figure 114. The ruins of of St. Dionysios

To the student of Classical Athens, the Areopagus means above all the meeting place of the Council of the Areopagus, the most venerable governing body and court of law in the city. That body certainly had its own council house *(bouleuterion)* somewhere on the hill, but its exact site has not yet been recognized. At times the Council held its meetings elsewhere, for instance in the Royal Stoa **㉖**. Thus we do not know with certainty where St. Paul stood when he was summoned before the Council to expound his faith. Local tradition, nevertheless, has always associated the Apostle with the hilltop. This is demonstrated above all by the establishment here of the Church of St. Dionysios, a member of the Council of the Areopagus who was Paul's most famous Athenian convert and the patron saint of Athens.

To reach the Church of St. Dionysios **㊾** we return to the Panathenaic Way and proceed upward almost to the saddle, and then turn right among the pine trees (Fig. 113). The ruins of the small basilica occupy a ledge at the foot of a vertical cliff (Fig. 114). To the west and north of the church are the remains of the Archbishop's Palace, which was connected with St. Dionysios through much of the 16th and 17th centuries. The last church on this site dated from the middle of the 16th century, but the presence of a number of graves of the 6th–7th centuries suggests the existence of a much earlier ecclesiastical building.

📖

Mycenaean tomb: T. L. Shear, *Hesperia* 9 (1940), pp. 274–291; *Agora* XIII (1971), pp. 158–169. **Geometric tomb**: E. L. Smithson, *Hesperia* 37 (1968), pp. 77–116; J. N. Coldstream, *Hesperia* 64 (1995), pp. 391–403. **Late houses**: A. Frantz, *PAPS* 119 (1975), pp. 34–38; J. McK. Camp II, *The Athenian Agora* (London, 1986), pp. 202–211; *Agora* XXIV (1988), pp. 37–48; *AgPicBk* 27 (2006), pp. 49–52. **Areopagus**: R. Wallace, *The Areopagos Council to 307 B.C.* (Baltimore, 1989). **Church of St. Dionysios**: E. W. Bodnar, J. Travlos, and A. Frantz, *Hesperia* 34 (1965), pp. 157–202.

Ⓝ Returning to the Agora proper, let us look at the series of buildings that closed its south side.

Figure 115. Nymphaion at the southeast corner of the Agora, 2nd century A.D. (Tentative restoration by S. Walker and N. Sunter)

⑥⓪ NYMPHAION

Partly beneath the Church of the Holy Apostles and partly exposed to the east are remains of a northward-facing, semicircular fountain house of the type commonly known as *nymphaia* from their resemblance to the cave sanctuaries of the Nymphs. Its most conspicuous remains are the heavy concrete foundations for the floor of a semicircular water basin and traces of three continuous steps and a parapet across the front (Fig. 115). Water was brought in from the southeast in a high-level aqueduct ⑤⑤. The great thickness of the outer wall suggests that its face was broken by niches for sculptures. Fragments of appropriate sculpture have been found nearby, among them a torso of the Venus Genetrix type in which a water pitcher has been substituted for the apple in the left hand of the goddess ⓜ. Pieces of marble revetment and carved architectural ornament attest to the rich adornment commonly found in *nymphaia* of the Roman period. In plan the building recalls the Exedra of Herodes at Olympia, the work of Herodes Atticus. The Athenian building, which drew its water from the aqueduct completed in A.D. 140, also dates from about the middle of the 2nd century.

📖

H. A. Thompson, *Hesperia* 24 (1955), pp. 57–59; *Agora* XIV (1972), pp. 202–203.

(61) THE ATHENIAN MINT

To the south of the Church of the Holy Apostles, and in part overlaid by both the church and the Nymphaion, are the remains of a large building from the end of the 5th century B.C. Rooms of various shapes and sizes were grouped along a large courtyard beneath which flowed the east branch of the Great Drain (Figs. 116, 117). Various pieces of evidence suggest that the building should be identified as the Mint *(argyrokopeion)*: the discovery on the floor of numerous blanks for the making of bronze coins, along with water basins and furnaces (Fig. 118). The evidence points to the minting of bronze coins in the 3rd and 2nd centuries B.C., but no evidence has come to light for the minting of silver, which must have occurred elsewhere. The building went out of use in the 1st century B.C., at a time when Athens ceased minting bronze coins.

J. McK. Camp II, *The Athenian Agora* (London, 1986), pp. 128–135; J. McK. Camp II and J. H. Kroll, *Hesperia* 70 (2001), pp. 127–162.

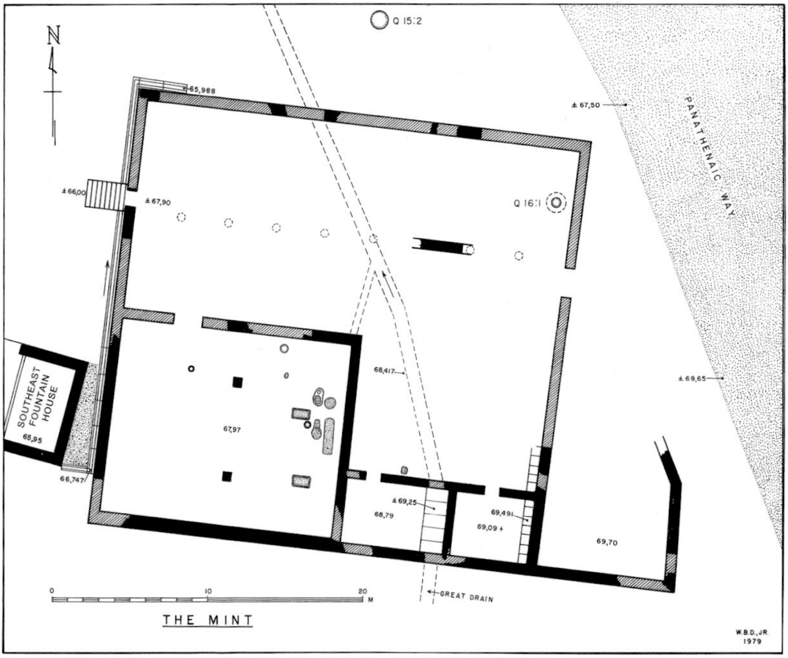

Figure 116. Restored plan of the remains of the Mint, ca. 400 B.C.

Figure 117. Aerial view of the area of the Mint, partially covered by the Church of the Holy Apostles. The blue line shows the course of the east branch of the Great Drain.

Figure 118. Bronze rod and coin blanks from the Mint, 3rd–2nd centuries B.C.

⑥₂ SOUTHEAST FOUNTAIN HOUSE

To the west of the Mint, and separated from it by a narrow alley, are the remains of a fountain house built in the second half of the 6th century B.C. The building was a long rectangle in plan, with its entry from the north (Figs. 119, 120). At either end was a shallow basin once floored with thin marble slabs. The walls of the building, at least in their lower parts, were constructed of carefully jointed Kara limestone; a Z-shaped clamp remains in place near the northeast corner. Water was delivered to a point at the middle of the back wall by a terracotta pipeline that entered the region of the Agora from the east, running beneath the ancient street (see Fig. 126). We may suppose that the water was conveyed in channels within the thickness of the wall to supply a series of spouts, doubtless in the shape of animal heads. From these ever-flowing spouts the girls of nearby households would have filled their water jugs, one of the most popular subjects among Athenian vase painters of the Late Archaic period. The overflow from the basins was carried off in a north-easterly direction, by means of an underground terracotta pipeline, to be used elsewhere (Fig. 121).

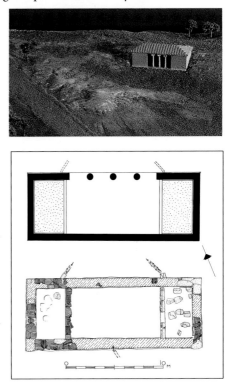

Figure 119 (above). Model of the Southeast Fountain House, view from the north

Figure 120 (below). Restored (top) and actual state (bottom) plans of the Southeast Fountain House, second half of the 6th century B.C.

This fountain house stood midway between the Odeion of Agrippa and the Eleusinion, that is, at the point where Pausanias in his account of the Agora (Paus. 1.14.1) mentioned the Enneakrounos, the "nine-spouted" fountain house erected by the tyrant Peisistratos or by his sons. Frequent references in the ancient authors leave no

Figure 121. Juncture of overflow pipes from the basins of the Southeast Fountain House, second half of the 6th century B.C.

doubt that the Enneakrounos was the most famous fountain house in Athens. Because of its great antiquity, its water was used for sacred purposes (e.g., for bathing before marriage). Although Pausanias believed this fountain house to be the nine-spouted one, Thucydides and other authors with greater probability place the Enneakrounos and the Kalirrhoe spring south of the Acropolis, in the bed of the Ilissos River.

Agora III (1957; reprinted 1973), nos. 434–455; Agora XIV (1972), pp. 197–199; J. McK. Camp II, *The Athenian Agora* (London, 1986), pp. 128–135; AgPicBk 26 (2006), pp. 6–8.

❻❸ CHURCH OF THE HOLY APOSTLES

The Church of the Holy Apostles, dating from about A.D. 1000, is the only monument now standing of the many buildings that covered the Agora in medieval times. After undergoing repeated alterations and enlargements through the centuries, the church was restored to its original form in the years 1954–1957 with the aid of a grant from the Samuel H. Kress Foundation of New York (Figs. 122, 123).

The plan of the church is a unique variant of the cross-in-square with apses at the ends of the four arms of the cross, the western apse being enclosed by a narthex (Fig. 124). Four columns help to support the dome. The outer walls are decorated with "kufic" ornament

Figure 122. Church of the Holy Apostles before restoration (1953), view from the southeast

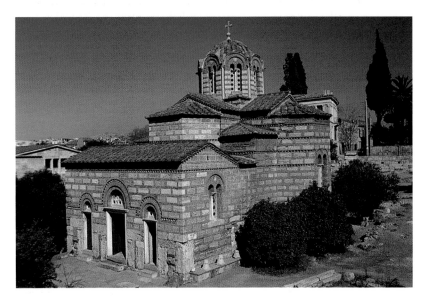

Figure 123. Church of the Holy Apostles today, view from the southwest

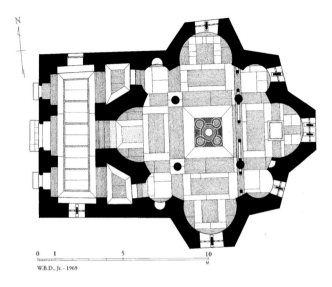

Figure 124. Plan of the Church of the Holy Apostles

(Arabic writing developed in the city of Kufa) in brickwork (Fig. 125). The altar, the altar screen, and the marble floor have been restored on the evidence of original fragments. The few wall paintings that have survived in the main body of the church date from the 17th cen-

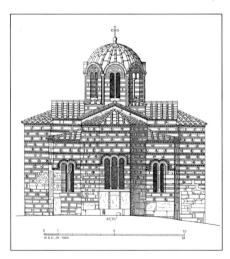

Figure 125. Church of the Holy Apostles, ca. 1000 A.D., east elevation

tury. On the walls of the narthex have been placed some contemporary paintings removed from the Chapel of St. Spyridon, which formerly stood above the Library of Pantainos **48**. Here too, in the left corridor, are a few fragments of painting from the Church of St. George in the Temple of Hephaistos **1**. The richly carved marble slab in the north end of the narthex is the front of a sarcophagus for which an alcove had been thrust out here early in the history of the church.

On shelves to the south of the Southeast Fountain House and on nearby walls have been assembled the more characteristic carved marbles of the early Christian and Byzantine periods found in the course of the Agora excavations.

AgPicBk 7 (1961); Agora XX (1971).

64 SOUTH STOA I

The remains of this building can best be viewed by ascending the stairway southwest of the Church of the Holy Apostles to the ancient street that bounded the south side of the Agora. Test trenches cut through the stratified road have shown that this had been an important thoroughfare at least since the Bronze Age. Its course determined the placing of all the early public buildings on the south side of the Agora (Fig. 126). The road surface has been restored to the level of the 5th and 4th centuries B.C.

South Stoa I was bisected diagonally and the western half destroyed by the building of South Stoa II. Enough survives, however, to permit the recovery of the design with fair assurance. The earlier building dates from the late 5th century B.C., and for two and a half centuries it dominated much of the Agora by virtue of its size and elevated site. The plan comprised a row of 15 rooms that shared a two-aisled colonnade, in front of which a terrace compensated for the terrain's downward

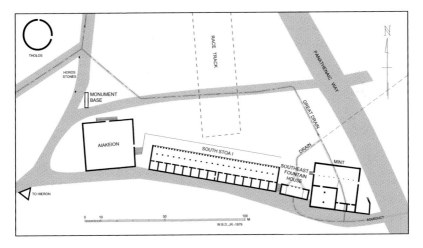

Figure 126. South side of the Agora in the late 5th century B.C.

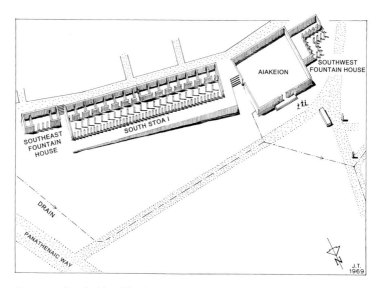

Figure 127. South side of the Agora, ca. 300 B.C.

slope toward north and west (Fig. 127). The interior walls were of sun-dried brick (Fig. 128) above socles of soft poros; the rear wall, now rebuilt, was entirely of stone since it served also as a retaining wall to support the roadway. The colonnade was also of poros; several stylobate blocks and a fragmentary Doric capital (now in storage) survive.

The rooms are closely uniform in size, and they are alike in having the front door set slightly off-center. The middle room is exceptional in that it was approached not directly from the porch like the other rooms but through a narrow anteroom to the east. This is an arrangement reminiscent of the dining suites in contemporary houses at Olynthos. The fifth room from the east in our building was floored in a way characteristic of dining rooms of the Classical period: a slightly raised border surfaced with pebble-studded cement encircled the room to support the wooden dining couches (Fig. 129). The eccentricity in the placement of the doorway is also an indication of dining rooms: it permitted the most economical distribution of dining couches of standard size. The rooms of South Stoa I would each have accommodated seven couches. In several cases a slight accumulation of ash in the middle of the room indicated the use of fire, probably in braziers, for heating or cooking. In a couple of the rooms benches of plastered clay had been built against the walls.

Figure 128. Mudbrick wall of South Stoa I (430–420 B.C.), as found

For the use of the building the most explicit clue is provided by an inscription of 221/20 B.C. found in the third room from the east. The text records the handing over of a set of official weights and measures by the commissioners of weights and measures (*metronomoi*) to their successors of the following year. The names of the five commissioners and their two secretaries are recorded. It appears probable that these commissioners had their headquarters in the building. There would have been room for a number of the other administrative boards of similar size that constituted the Athenian civil service. In addition to providing office space, the stoa would also have offered dining accommodations in which the officials could take their

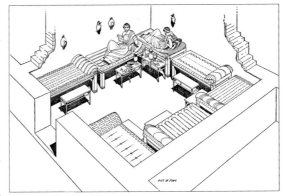

Figure 129. Restoration of dining room with seven couches

midday meals together. Note that the dining room accommodated seven men, just the number of members attested for the board of *metronomoi* including secretaries.

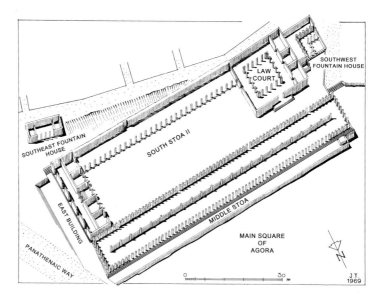

H. A. Thompson, *Hesperia* 37 (1968), pp. 43–56, 73–76; *Agora* XIV (1972), pp. 74–78; J. McK. Camp II, *The Athenian Agora* (London, 1986), pp. 122–126.

65–70 SOUTH SQUARE

We now turn to the examination of a complex of buildings that bordered the south side of the main square of the Agora, which for want of an ancient name we may designate as the South Square. This lesser square took shape in the course of the second and third quarters of the 2nd century B.C. through the construction of the Middle Stoa, the East Building, and South Stoa II, in that sequence (Fig. 130). The purpose of these buildings is problematic; among numerous suggestions, perhaps a commercial function is the most probable.

Near the middle of the South Square are the slight remains, consisting of a few scattered foundation stones, of two buildings; both of these, to judge from their plans, were temples. The eastern building was clearly peripteral (with columns on all four sides); the western

Figure 130. South Square after Hellenistic additions, ca. 140 B.C.

had a broad cella with a porch only on its east end. Both date from the Hellenistic period, probably the late 2nd century B.C., and both appear to have suffered in the Roman siege of 86 B.C. We have as yet no clue to the divinity worshipped in either temple.

South Square: *Agora* XIV (1972), pp. 65–71; J. McK. Camp II, *The Athenian Agora* (London, 1986), pp. 175–179.

For convenience in viewing the remains of the various buildings, we will proceed in an order the reverse of the sequence of their construction. We begin therefore with South Stoa II, and to see it to better advantage we go back down the steps toward the front of the Church of the Holy Apostles and then down a second flight.

65 SOUTH STOA II

South Stoa II was a simple one-aisled colonnade comprising 30 columns of the Doric order supported on two steps. Setting marks for two of the columns are preserved at the east end of the stoa. The original rear wall was of large, regular limestone blocks with a backing of conglomerate. Near the middle of the back wall was an arched niche for a fountain. The water came from a great stone aqueduct beneath the street to the south of the stoa; it poured into a basin formed by a parapet across the front of the niche (Figs. 131, 132).

The facade of the stoa was of reused material taken from the Square Peristyle at the northeast corner of the Agora 44 when that building was demolished to make way for the Stoa of Attalos; this applies to steps, columns, and entablature. The evidence for reuse is especially clear in the case of the steps; on their tops are numerous

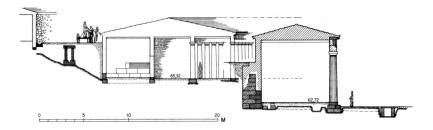

Figure 131. Cross section, showing relationship (left to right) of the street bordering the Agora on the south, the aqueduct (below street), South Stoa I, and South Stoa II

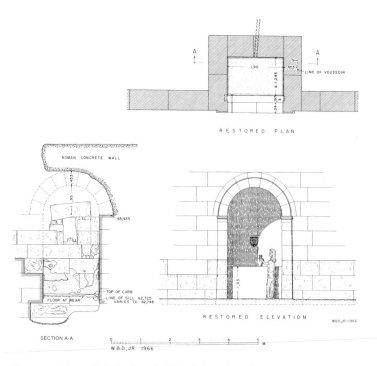

Figure 132. Fountain in back wall of South Stoa II, 2nd century B.C.

traces of superimposed blocks in places where such blocks could not have existed in the present building. Elsewhere on the tops of the steps in the eastern part of the stoa are incised a number of large letters of the Greek alphabet. These too date from the first period of the building, at which time there would appear to have been one letter between each pair of columns, presumably a system of numbering the bays of the colonnade. On top of the back wall of the stoa toward its east end have been placed two blocks from the entablature of the Square Peristyle: one from the triglyph and metope frieze, one from the cornice. These members had been reused elsewhere in the Agora; they are displayed here to illustrate the entablature that was employed, at second hand, in South Stoa II. They are cut from a distinctive kind of travertine, and the workmanship is worthy of the period when they were made.

South Stoa II suffered in the Roman siege of 86 B.C. and was subsequently dismantled. Industry intruded into the desolate area and flourished in the 1st and early part of the 2nd centuries A.D. Great quantities of slag from the smelting of iron and chips from the working of marble were found in the excavation. In the 2nd century A.D., probably in the time of Hadrian (A.D. 117–138), the industrialists were banished and the area was cleaned up. At this time the rear wall of the stoa was rebuilt with a backing of concrete, of which a long section remains in the middle part of the building, apparently to support an aqueduct carrying water westward to a large bath complex.

📖

H. A. Thompson, *Hesperia* 29 (1960), pp. 359–363.

66 EAST BUILDING

The east end of South Stoa II was built against the front of a small, slightly earlier structure with a north–south orientation, known as the East Building. This earlier building was evidently designed to close the east end of the new square; it seems also to have served as its formal entrance.

The building was approached by way of a broad terrace along the whole of its east front. A wide flight of steps led down to the terrace from the east, and a narrow stairway from the south. The front foundation of the building is too narrow to have supported a colonnade; it is to be restored rather with a wall broken by several, perhaps five, doorways. The interior was divided into two parts by a wall on its median line. The west half comprised five compartments, whereas the east was a single long hall.

The eastern room was floored with marble-chip mosaic in which were set a number of low marble bases about 0.90 m square. Four of these bases remain and the series is to be restored as 12 in all, divided into two groups of six, separated by an open interval on the axis of the building. In the top of each base are four shallow square sockets; presumably they served to retain in a fixed position some piece of wooden furniture with four legs, such as a table (Fig. 133).

Of the five compartments in the west half of the building, the central one certainly contained a stairway by which one descended from the higher level on the east to the lower level of the South Square, the difference being about 1.70 m. The next room to the south is to be restored, from indications in the foundations, as an exedra with two columns in its front and a marble bench around its other three

Figure 133. Detail of the floor of the East Building, show-ing the marble slabs with cuttings for the attachment of wooden furniture, 2nd century B.C.

sides. The southernmost room was provided with water that issued from spouts set in the face of the wall. The two northern rooms are too ruinous to permit restoration.

Agora XIV (1972), pp. 68–70.

67 MIDDLE STOA

We move on to the Middle Stoa, the earliest and largest unit in the building program of the 2nd century B.C. that resulted in the South Square. Let us start at the east end, where the fabric of the building is best preserved.

With a length of some 147 m and width of about 17.50 m, the Middle Stoa, in terms of ground plan, was much the largest building of the Agora. On all four sides it was enclosed by colonnades of unfluted Doric columns, 160 in all (Fig. 134). The stumps of three of these columns still stand in situ above the canonical three steps at the east end of the stoa; many more drums, recovered from the Post-Herulian

Figure 134. Middle Stoa and South Square of the 2nd century B.C., as seen from the upper floor of the Stoa of Attalos

Wall, have been set up around the building. The structure was divided longitudinally into two equal aisles by a row of 23 interior columns with intervening screen walls. These inner columns were presumably Ionic, but nothing of this order has yet been recognized.

A close examination of the three column stumps at the east end of the stoa will reveal traces of a thin parapet between the columns. Dowel holes in about one-half of the surviving outer column drums indicate that similar parapets enclosed a considerable proportion of the total periphery of the stoa; they were presumably confined to certain lengths at each end of the building. The parapets rose only about three-quarters of the height of the columns and were crowned with a nicely profiled capping course. The open space above admitted light and air.

The north facade of the stoa was flanked by a terrace of generous width. Since the ground sloped gently down from east to west, this terrace through most of its length lay well above the floor level of the main square and therefore commanded a splendid view across the Agora. Toward the west the terrace stopped short of the end of the building proper so as to minimize interference with the flow of traffic through the southwest entrance to the Agora.

Figure 135. Doric entablature of the Middle Stoa, 2nd century B.C.

The south flank of the stoa was bordered by a marble gutter, of which a little remains in place at the east end.

Apart from the columns, little of the superstructure of the stoa has survived. Several of its epistyles, made of poros from Piraeus, have been placed on the outer edge of the terrace near its east end; the backs of the blocks have suffered greatly from the fire that destroyed the building in A.D. 267. A few fragments of the frieze (in storage) indicated that the triglyphs were of fine-grained Aeginetan poros painted blue, while the metopes were of white marble. The terracotta sima showed foliage in relief between the lions' heads, the whole richly painted (Fig. 135). Although the architectural forms are simple and the materials modest, the workmanship throughout is of a high order; evidently the project was supported with ample means. The construction of the main part of the Middle Stoa falls in the first half of the 2nd century B.C.

H. A. Thompson, *Hesperia* 21 (1952), pp. 86–90; J. Travlos, *Pictorial Dictionary of Ancient Athens* (London, 1971), pp. 234–239; *Agora* XIV (1972), pp. 66–68; V. R. Grace, *Hesperia* 54 (1985), pp. 1–54.

68 AIAKEION

The large rectangular structure erected in the 6th century B.C. on high ground at the south side of the square balanced the predecessor of the Tholos and the Old Bouleuterion on the west side. The site of the building is now sadly desolate. The best-preserved part is the stepped foundation of the north wall. After examining this, the visitor will do well to climb the modern stairs to the high road south of the building, whence one can distinguish the outline of the foundations that have been filled out with modern masonry.

In its original form the building consisted of an enclosure open to the sky, approaching a square in plan and measuring internally about 26.50 × 31 m. The enclosing wall was built of well-squared blocks of Aeginetan poros crowned by a double cornice. The exact height cannot be determined, but the thickness of the wall (0.48 m) and the delicate treatment of the molding on the soffit of the cornice suggest that it was higher than a man's head. The principal entrance was in the middle of the north side; there was a lesser doorway in the east side. Because of the downward slope of the land, three steps were set against the middle part of the north front, perhaps in connection with some more monumental treatment of the entrance. The clay floor inside the enclosure was made to slope gently toward the northeast corner, from which point the surface water was carried off in a large stone drain.

The building has been assigned various identities in the past, but a passage in Herodotos (5.89) and an inscription (I 7557) of the 4th century B.C. would now seem to confirm its identification as the Aiakeion, a sanctuary of an Aeginetan hero, founded in Athens at the behest of the oracle at Delphi. It fulfills all the criteria demanded by the two sources: it is in the Agora, was in use both before and after the Persian destruction, and is large enough to have been used to store several thousand bushels of grain.

In the course of its long existence the building underwent many alterations, of which only the principal can be noted here. Around the middle of the 2nd century B.C. a complete peristyle was inserted, and the building would seem to have been roofed with a lantern to provide light and air while assuring privacy. This building, along with its neighbors, suffered greatly in the Roman siege of 86 B.C. A number of stone catapult balls were found in its ruins. It was subsequently occupied by small industrial establishments: a potter's kiln and a marble-working shop.

Agora III (1957; reprinted 1973), nos. 103, 104; *Hesperia* Suppl. 29 (1998).

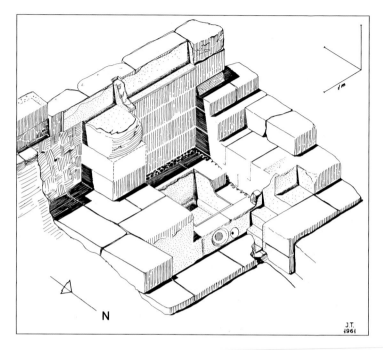

Figure 136. Drawing of remains of the waterclock (klepsydra), *late 4th century B.C.*

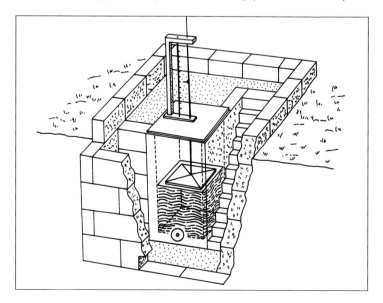

Figure 137. Restored drawing of the waterclock

(69) WATERCLOCK

Against the north facade of the Aiakeion, toward its northwest corner, are the clearly visible remains of a monumental waterclock dating from the late 4th century B.C. Water, drawn from the aqueduct supplying the Southwest Fountain House, was made to fill a stone-lined vertical shaft, the bottom of which was sunk deep below ground level (Fig. 136). The water was then allowed to escape through a very small aperture low down in the wall of the shaft. The falling water level, perhaps by means of a float, must have activated a pointer to indicate the passing hours (Fig. 137). In the 3rd century B.C., following advances made in Alexandria, the tank was modified to serve as a more sophisticated in-flow rather than out-flow clock. As a public timepiece the installation was well placed, close to one of the principal entrances to the Agora. It was dismantled in the 2nd century B.C., at the time the waterclock in the Tower of the Winds was constructed several hundred meters to the east.

J. E. Armstrong and J. McK. Camp II, *Hesperia* 46 (1977), pp. 147–161.

(70) SOUTHWEST FOUNTAIN HOUSE

To the west of the Aiakeion are the foundations of a once splendid public facility, which for want of an ancient name we may designate as the Southwest Fountain House (Fig. 138). The building probably dates to the third quarter of the 4th century B.C. It underwent modifications in the later 4th and the 2nd centuries B.C., was destroyed in the siege of 86 B.C., was subsequently stripped to its lowest foundations, and was never rebuilt.

The fountain house was well situated, for it made abundant fresh water readily available to those entering and leaving the Agora and also to the resident population in the densely inhabited area around the southwest corner of the public place. It was set deep into the bedrock in order to conform with the level of the supply line, and this circumstance, no doubt, kept both the building and its water cool.

The water came from the east in a great stone aqueduct that ran under the street bordering the south side of the Agora and was delivered to the southeast corner of the fountain. It is worthwhile to peer through the iron grating at the southwest corner of the Aiakeion in order to see a section of the ancient aqueduct. The channel was very

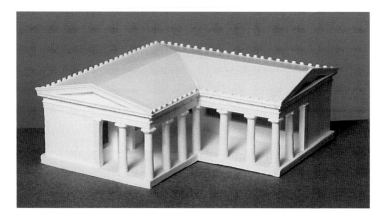

Figure 138. Model of the Southwest Fountain House, one of the largest in Athens, ca. 350–325 B.C.

solidly constructed of large slabs of soft poros laid horizontally for floor and roof, vertically for the walls. The water flowed in a small trench, semicircular in section, cut in the floor. The open channel above this, 0.45 m wide and 1.20 m high, was large enough to permit the passage of a workman engaged in cleaning or repairing.

The fountain house itself was L-shaped. An inner row of columns divided the building into two parts: a basin and a porch. The front of the basin consisted of a parapet of hard poros set between the inner columns; over this the water was drawn. A small surviving fragment from the top of a parapet is deeply worn by the pitchers. On the stylobate of the porch are traces of column bases 0.66 m in diameter, but nothing remains either of the columns or of the entablature.

The fountain house was soon enlarged by the construction of an annex at its southwest corner. Water was supplied by the westward extension of the great stone aqueduct. In the annex one could approach the wall from which the water issued and hold one's pitcher directly below the spout: a more satisfactory arrangement than dipping one's drinking water from a basin as in the main building. At a later date, probably in the 2nd century B.C., the southwest annex was abandoned in favor of a similar installation at the northeast corner of the original building.

Agora XIV (1972), pp. 200–201; J. McK. Camp II, *The Athenian Agora* (London, 1986), pp. 156–157.

(71) TRIANGULAR SHRINE

Proceeding up the ancient road to the west of the Southwest Fountain House and under the branches of a wild pistachio tree, we come to an important traffic intersection. From this point radiated roads going northeast to the Agora, southwest toward the Pnyx, west toward the Piraeus Gate, east to the southern border of the Agora, and southeast to the northern slope of the Areopagus. For the most part these ancient streets are narrow, irregular, and roughly surfaced with gravel. Almost all of them are underlain by drains and water channels that show countless repairs and adjustments. The most impressive is the road that bordered the south side of the Agora. Its well-kept gravel surface maintains a fairly uniform width of about 6 m; along its south side ran a gutter to carry off the surface water from the higher ground above.

In the angle between the two roads coming from the east one will recognize the remains of a triangular enclosure once surrounded by a low wall of polygonal limestone masonry (Fig. 139). Its sanctity is attested by an inscription on a marble post set against the face of the enclosure wall at the east end of the north side. The text reads "Of the Sanctuary" *(tou hierou)* in lettering of the latter part of the 5th century B.C. The ceramic evidence supports a date in this period for the construction of the triangular enclosure. A mass of rough masonry found

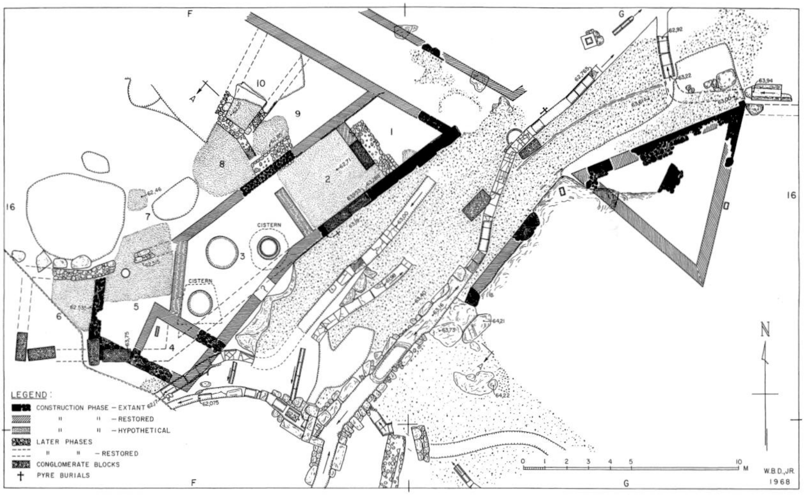

Figure 139. Plan of the Triangular Shrine, 5th century B.C. (right), and sculptor's house, 5th–3rd century B.C. (left)

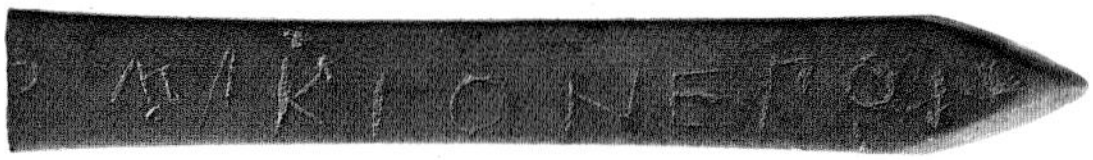

Figure 140. Bone stylus inscribed with the name of the sculptor Mikion

at a lower level inside the enclosure in a context of the 7th century B.C. suggests that this had been a sacred spot much earlier.

Just to the west lie the remains of a house of the Classical and Hellenistic periods where a sculptor named Mikion once worked, as we know from a bone stylus inscribed with his name (Fig. 140).

Triangular Shrine: H. A Thompson, *Hesperia* 37 (1968), pp. 58–60; G. Lalonde, *Hesperia* 37 (1968), pp. 123–133. **Sculptor's house**: T. L. Shear Jr., *Hesperia* 38 (1969), pp. 383–394; S. G. Miller, *Hesperia* 43 (1974), pp. 194–245; *AgPicBk* 27 (2006), pp. 17–19.

(72) STATE PRISON(?)

About 60 m to the southwest of the Triangular Shrine is a building of unusual plan. A long, narrow structure built in the mid-5th century B.C., it was entered at its north end from an important ancient street leading northwestward toward the Piraeus Gate. The plan comprised two rows of square rooms, five in one, three in the other, separated and served by a corridor leading south to a large open courtyard (Figs. 141, 142). Incorporated in the northeast corner of the building is a semidetached unit consisting of four rooms. Many features of the building are appropriate to a commercial/industrial complex, though its identification as the State Prison *(desmoterion)* has also been proposed.

The state prison of Athens is best known from the casual references to it in Plato's *Phaedo.* This dialogue tells of the month Sokrates spent in prison between his condemnation and his execution by drinking hemlock (399 B.C.). Our structure appears to satisfy the requirements, being close to the Agora, adjacent to an important street, and of appropriate date and plan. In the northwestern room were found a large water jar and a basin set in the floor; such facilities may have served for the bath Sokrates took before drinking the poison. In the ruins of the building were found 13 small terracotta bottles of a type certainly used in antiquity for drugs, which perhaps in this case may have been intended to hold the powerful and

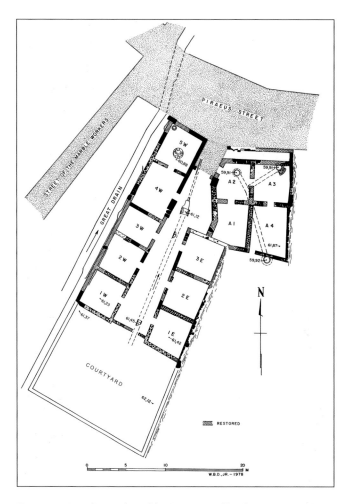

Figure 141. Actual state plan of the State Prison(?), 5th century B.C. Room 5W may have been used for bathing; room A3 contained the cistern with terracotta medicine bottles.

carefully measured juice of the hemlock plant (Fig. 143). It may not be entirely by chance that the ruins also yielded a small marble portrait, probably to be identified as Sokrates (Fig. 144).

M. Crosby, *Hesperia* 20 (1951), pp. 168–187; *Agora* III (1957; reprinted 1973), pp. 149–150; E. Vanderpool, *From Athens to Gordion* (Philadelphia, 1980), pp. 17–31.

Fig. 142. The State Prison(?) seen from the north, 5th century B.C.

Figure 143. Set of 13 clay medicine bottles, 4th century B.C.

*Figure 144.
Fragmentary
marble statuette
possibly of Sokrates,
4th century B.C.*

(73) BATH AT NORTHWEST FOOT OF THE AREOPAGUS

Prominent above and to the east of the State Prison(?) are the extensive remains of a bathing establishment with a history that extended in five major phases from the late 2nd century B.C. into the late 6th century A.D. Characteristic of its earliest phase was a round room in which some 20 stone bathtubs could have been placed radially against the enclosing wall; one of these tubs is now shown on the terrace of the Stoa of Attalos. The irregularities of the terrain and the many vicissitudes suffered by the building resulted in a very informal plan in striking variance from that of the normal bath of the Roman period (Fig. 145). The most readily recognizable element of the later phases is a large expanse of marble-chip floor at a high level; this belonged to the dressing room *(apodyterion)*. To the south is a large cistern for the storage of water.

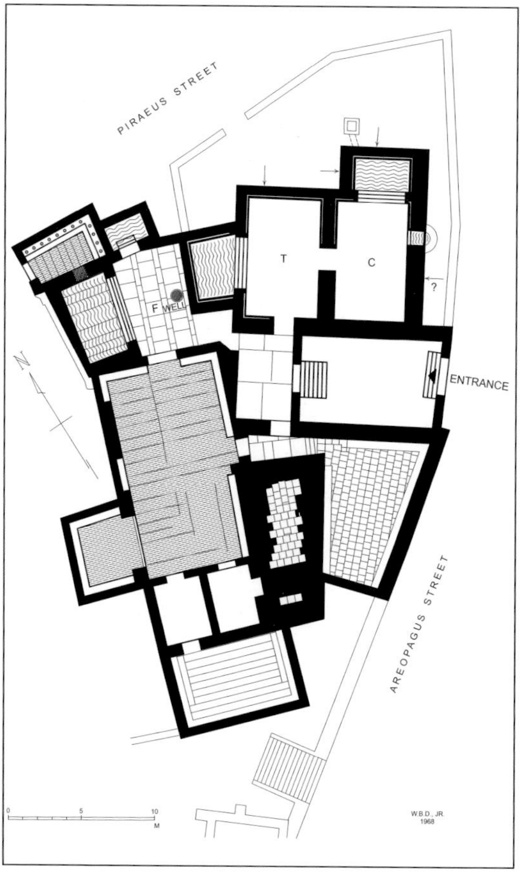

Figure 145. Plan of the Hellenistic/Roman bath, 2nd century B.C.–6th century A.D. Last phase shown here.

T. L. Shear Jr., *Hesperia* 38 (1969), pp. 394–415.

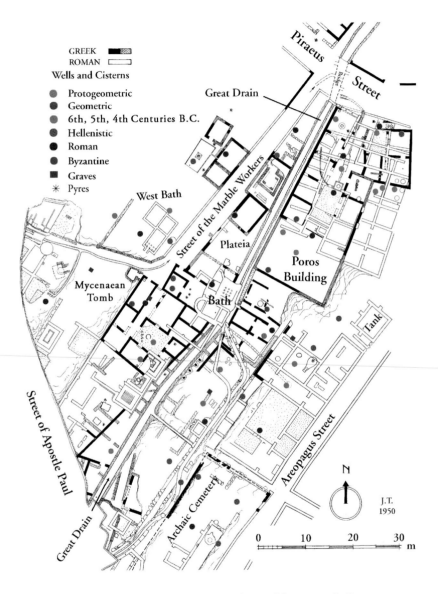

Figure 146. The residential-industrial district southwest of the Agora. The "Poros Building" (center right) is another name given to the building tentatively identified as the State Prison. The other walls and wells represent private houses dating from the 5th century B.C. to the Byzantine period.

74 RESIDENTIAL-INDUSTRIAL AREA TO WEST AND SOUTH OF THE AREOPAGUS

The extensive excavations to the west of the Areopagus were begun with a view to finding a site for the Agora Museum. The wealth of ancient remains that came to light necessitated a change of plan and led to the reconstruction of the Stoa of Attalos to serve as a museum. The removal of vast quantities of silt, which reached a maximum depth of 12 m, revealed a shallow valley between the Areopagus and the Hill of the Nymphs (now crowned by the National Observatory). This valley was drained by the west branch of the Great Drain. In addition to such public buildings as the Prison(?) and the Bath, the area had been throughout most of antiquity a thickly settled residential-industrial district (Fig. 146). In the bottom of the valley toward the southwest may be traced the foundations of several houses of the 5th and 4th centuries B.C. The typical plan comprised a number of rooms grouped around a courtyard with a well near its middle (Fig. 147). Both construction and furnishings were modest: walls of rubble masonry, floors of clay, no mosaics, very few columns. These were presumably the dwellings of artisans who carried on their activities either within their own houses or in nearby shops of still more modest appearance.

Casting pits for the making of bronze statues have been found in the area, one of the 4th and one of the 2nd century B.C. (both have been refilled). Great quantities of marble chips attest to the carving of sculpture, especially in the 5th and 4th centuries B.C., while molds for the making of terracotta figurines of Hellenistic types show that coroplasts were also busy in the area.

In the Roman period the hill slopes both east and west of the valley were occupied by large dwelling houses. Their walls were painted in simple paneled schemes, and a few of the rooms were floored with mosaic. Most of these houses suffered in the Herulian sack of A.D. 267, but some were rebuilt to continue in use into the 6th century. Here as elsewhere in the area of the Agora the earliest remains are burials. Two small chamber tombs of the Mycenaean period came to light near the bottom of the valley, and a family cemetery comprising 48 burials ranging in date from the 8th through the 6th centuries B.C. has been explored on the west slope of the Areopagus.

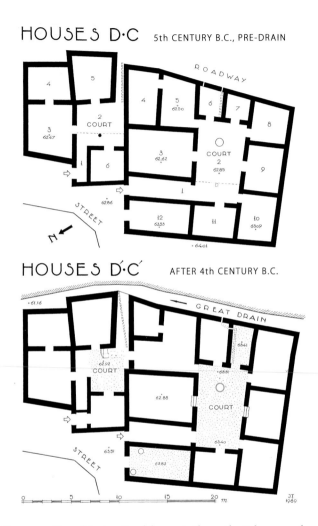

Figure 147. Plan of the two Greek houses in the residential area south of the State Prison(?), 5th and 4th centuries B.C.

To the south of the Areopagus, excavations in the 1890s by the German Archaeological Institute revealed the continuation of the residential area: an ancient roadway bordered by close-set houses and small shrines, notably the Amyneion, seat of a healing cult.

R. S. Young, *Hesperia* 20 (1951), pp. 67–288; *Agora* XIV (1972), pp. 15–18, 173–191.

List of
Publications

LIST OF PUBLICATIONS CONCERNING THE ATHENIAN AGORA PUBLISHED BY THE AMERICAN SCHOOL OF CLASSICAL STUDIES AT ATHENS

THE ATHENIAN AGORA: RESULTS OF EXCAVATIONS CONDUCTED BY THE AMERICAN SCHOOL OF CLASSICAL STUDIES AT ATHENS

A series of scholarly monographs on the final results of the excavations.

I E. B. Harrison, *Portrait Sculpture* (1953).

II M. Thompson, *Coins: From the Roman through the Venetian Period* (1954).

III R. E. Wycherley, *Literary and Epigraphical Testimonia* (1957; reprinted 1973).

IV R. H. Howland, *Greek Lamps and Their Survivals* (1958; reprinted 1966).

V H. S. Robinson, *Pottery of the Roman Period: Chronology* (1959).

VI C. Grandjouan, *Terracottas and Plastic Lamps of the Roman Period* (1961).

VII J. Perlzweig, *Lamps of the Roman Period: First to Seventh Century after Christ* (1961; reprinted 1971).

VIII E. T. H. Brann, *Late Geometric and Protoattic Pottery: Mid-8th to Late 7th Century B.C.* (1962; reprinted 1971).

IX G. C. Miles, *The Islamic Coins* (1962).

X M. Lang and M. Crosby, *Weights, Measures, and Tokens* (1964).

XI E. B. Harrison, *Archaic and Archaistic Sculpture* (1965).

XII B. A. Sparkes and L. Talcott, *Black and Plain Pottery of the 6th, 5th, and 4th Centuries B.C.* (1970).

XIII S. A. Immerwahr, *The Neolithic and Bronze Ages* (1971).

XIV H. A. Thompson and R. E. Wycherley, *The Agora of Athens: The History, Shape, and Uses of an Ancient City Center* (1972).

XV B. D. Meritt and J. S. Traill, *Inscriptions: The Athenian Councillors* (1974).

XVI A. G. Woodhead, *Inscriptions: The Decrees* (1997).

XVII D. W. Bradeen, *Inscriptions: The Funerary Monuments* (1974).

XIX G. V. Lalonde, M. K. Langdon, and M. B. Walbank, *Inscriptions: Horoi, Poletai Records, and Leases of Public Lands* (1991).

XX   A. Frantz, *The Church of the Holy Apostles* (1971).

XXI   M. Lang, *Graffiti and Dipinti* (1976).

XXII   S. I. Rotroff, *Hellenistic Pottery: Athenian and Imported Mold-made Bowls* (1982).

XXIII   M. B. Moore and M. Z. P. Philippides, *Attic Black-Figured Pottery* (1986).

XXIV   A. Frantz, *Late Antiquity: A.D. 267–700* (1988).

XXV   M. Lang, *Ostraka* (1990).

XXVI   J. H. Kroll, with A. S. Walker, *The Greek Coins* (1993).

XXVII   R. F. Townsend, *The East Side of the Agora: The Remains beneath the Stoa of Attalos* (1995).

XXVIII   A. L. Boegehold et al., *The Lawcourts at Athens: Sites, Buildings, Equipment, Procedure, and Testimonia* (1995).

XXIX   S. I. Rotroff, *Hellenistic Pottery: Athenian and Imported Wheelmade Table Ware and Related Material* (1997).

XXX   M. B. Moore, *Attic Red-Figured and White-Ground Pottery* (1997).

XXXI   M. M. Miles, *The City Eleusinion* (1998).

XXXII   J. W. Hayes, *Roman Pottery: Fine-Ware Imports* (2008).

XXXIII   S. I. Rotroff, *Hellenistic Pottery: The Plain Wares* (2006).

XXXIV   G. D. Weinberg and E. M. Stern, *Vessel Glass* (2009).

ATHENIAN AGORA PICTURE BOOKS

Short thematic surveys (32–50 pages) with numerous illustrations and a brief text. Those marked with an * are also available in Modern Greek.

1.   B. A. Sparkes and L. Talcott, *Pots and Pans of Classical Athens* (1959).

2.   H. A. Thompson, *The Stoa of Attalos II in Athens* (revised 1992).

3.   D. B. Thompson, *Miniature Sculpture from the Athenian Agora* (1959).

4.*   M. Lang, *The Athenian Citizen: Democracy in the Athenian Agora* (revised 2004).

5.   E. B. Harrison, *Ancient Portraits from the Athenian Agora* (1960).

6.   V. R. Grace, *Amphoras and the Ancient Wine Trade* (revised 1979).

7.   A. Frantz, *The Middle Ages in the Athenian Agora* (1961).

8. D. B. Thompson and R. E. Griswold, *Garden Lore of Ancient Athens* (1963).

9. J. Perlzweig, *Lamps from the Athenian Agora* (1963).

10. B. D. Meritt, *Inscriptions from the Athenian Agora* (1966).

11. M. Lang, *Waterworks in the Athenian Agora* (1968).

12. D. B. Thompson, *An Ancient Shopping Center: The Athenian Agora* (revised 1993).

13. S. A. Immerwahr, *Early Burials from the Agora Cemeteries* (1973).

14. M. Lang, *Graffiti in the Athenian Agora* (revised 1988).

15. F. S. Kleiner, *Greek and Roman Coins in the Athenian Agora* (1975).

16.* J. McK. Camp II, *The Athenian Agora: A Short Guide* (revised 2003).

17. M. Lang, *Socrates in the Agora* (1978).

18. F. S. Kleiner, *Mediaeval and Modern Coins in the Athenian Agora* (1978).

19. J. McK. Camp II, *Gods and Heroes in the Athenian Agora* (1980).

20. C. C. Mattusch, *Bronzeworkers in the Athenian Agora* (1982).

21. J. McK. Camp II and W. B. Dinsmoor Jr., *Ancient Athenian Building Methods* (1984).

22. R. D. Lamberton and S. I. Rotroff, *Birds of the Athenian Agora* (1985).

23. M. Lang, *Life, Death, and Litigation in the Athenian Agora* (1994).

24. J. McK. Camp II, *Horses and Horsemanship in the Athenian Agora* (1998).

25. J. Neils and S. V. Tracy, *The Games at Athens* (2003).

26. S. I. Rotroff and R. D. Lamberton, *Women in the Athenian Agora* (2006).

27. C. Lawton, *Marbleworkers in the Athenian Agora* (2006).

HESPERIA SUPPLEMENTS

Issued at irregular intervals in the same format as *Hesperia*. Volumes concerning Agora material are:

1. S. Dow, *Prytaneis: A Study of the Inscriptions Honoring the Athenian Councillors* (1937).

2. R. S. Young, *Late Geometric Graves and a Seventh-Century Well in the Agora* (1939).

4. H. A. Thompson, *The Tholos of Athens and Its Predecessors* (1940).

5. W. B. Dinsmoor, *Observations on the Hephaisteion* (1941).

8. *Commemorative Studies in Honor of Theodore Leslie Shear* (1949).

9. J. V. A. Fine, *Horoi: Studies in Mortgage, Real Security, and Land Tenure in Ancient Athens* (1951).

12. D. J. Geagan, *The Athenian Constitution after Sulla* (1967).

13. J. H. Oliver, *Marcus Aurelius: Aspects of Civic and Cultural Policy in the East* (1970).

14. J. S. Traill, *The Political Organization of Attica* (1975).

17. T. L. Shear Jr., *Kallias of Sphettos and the Revolt of Athens in 286 B.C.* (1978).

19. *Studies in Attic Epigraphy, History, and Topography Presented to Eugene Vanderpool* (1982).

20. *Studies in Athenian Architecture, Sculpture, and Topography Presented to Homer A. Thompson* (1982).

22. E. J. Walters, *Attic Grave Reliefs That Represent Women in the Dress of Isis* (1988).

23. C. Grandjouan, *Hellenistic Relief Molds from the Athenian Agora* (1989).

25. S. I. Rotroff and J. H. Oakley, *Debris from a Public Dining Place in the Athenian Agora* (1992).

29. R. S. Stroud, *The Athenian Grain-Tax Law of 374/3 B.C.* (1998).

31. J. K. Papadopoulos, *Ceramicus Redivivus: The Early Iron Age Potters' Field in the Area of the Classical Athenian Agora* (2003).

38. M. B. Walbank, *Fragmentary Decrees from the Athenian Agora* (2008).

OTHER BOOKS

C. A. Mauzy, *Agora Excavations, 1931–2006: A Pictorial History* (2006).

J. K. Papadopoulos, *The Art of Antiquity: Piet de Jong and the Athenian Agora* (2007).

INDEX

Numbers in **Bold** = main entry or description
* = ancient literary source

CAPTIONS AND CREDITS

Page 6: Hephaisteion of the Athenian Agora

Pages 8–9: Top row, left to right, from the Alison Frantz Archive, ASCSA
Lion Gate at Mycenae, detail of lions; Moschophoros (Calf-Bearer); Parthenon
from northwest; Temple of Olympian Zeus, Athens; Arch of Hadrian, Athens;
Church of the Holy Apostles, detail of dome.

Pages 8–9: Bottom row, left to right
Enthroned goddess figurine, Mycenaean; boundary stone of the Agora,
ca. 500 B.C.; bronze head of Nike, ca. 400 B.C.; lower colonnade of the Stoa of
Attalos, ca. 150 B.C.; portrait head of Roman imperial priest, ca. 200 A.D.;
plate with sgraffito decoration, 12th century (watercolor by Piet de Jong)

Page 12: Upper floor of the Stoa of Attalos, watercolor by Piet de Jong

Page 28: A view of the Athenian Agora toward the southeast from the
Hephaisteion in 1949

Page 34: Panorama of the Agora site in 2002, looking east

Unless otherwise noted, all photographs are courtesy of the Agora Excavations.